THE STORY OF DAVID & GOLIATH

Activity Book

The story of David & Goliath Activity Book

All rights reserved. By purchasing this Activity Book, the buyer is permitted to copy the activity sheets for personal and classroom use only, but not for commercial resale. With the exception of the above, this Activity Book may not be reproduced in whole or in part in any manner without written permission of the publisher.

Bible Pathway Adventures® is a trademark of BPA Publishing Ltd.
Defenders of the Faith® is a trademark of BPA Publishing Ltd.

ISBN: 978-1-7771601-4-2

Author: Pip Reid

Creative Director: Curtis Reid

For more Bible resources, including Activity Books and printables, visit our website at:

www.biblepathwayadventures.com

◇ Introduction ◇

Your children will LOVE learning about the story of David and Goliath through *The Story of David & Goliath Activity Book*. It's packed with ready-to-go lessons, coloring pages, fun worksheets, and puzzles to help educators just like you teach children a Biblical faith. Includes scripture references for easy Bible verse look-up and a handy answer key for guidance and clarity.

Bible Pathway Adventures helps educators teach children a Biblical faith in a fun and creative way. We do this via our Activity Books and printable activities – available on our website: www.biblepathwayadventures.com

Thank you for buying this Activity Book and supporting our ministry. Every book purchased helps us continue our work providing free discipleship resources to families and missions around the world.

The search for Truth is more fun than Tradition!

Table of Contents

Introduction 3

Lesson One: David is anointed king 6
Coloring page: Saul spares King Agag 8
Worksheet: Who were the Amalekites? 9
Worksheet: Saul spares King Agag 10
Bible quiz: The prophet Samuel 11
Worksheet: The prophet Samuel 12
Worksheet: David the shepherd 13
Newspaper worksheet: David anointed king! 14
Worksheet: David is chosen king 15
Worksheet: Discovering Bethlehem 16
Worksheet: Jesse's family 17

Lesson Two: David works for King Saul 18
Bible word search puzzle: David works for King Saul 20
Worksheet: What did the Israelites wear? 21
Maze activity: Help David visit King Saul 22
Creative writing: David's hardworking helper 23
Let's learn Hebrew: David 24
Worksheet: Who was King Saul? 26
Coloring page: David plays the lyre 27
Map activity: Tribe of Benjamin 28
Worksheet: David plays the lyre 29
Worksheet: David and his lyre 30
Creative writing: King Saul 31

Lesson Three: Facing Goliath 32
Bible quiz: Facing Goliath 34
Coloring page: Goliath 35
Worksheets: The Nephilim 36
Worksheet: Match the scriptures 38
Map activity: Valley of Elah 39
Worksheet: Valley of Elah 40
Worksheet: How big was Goliath? 41
Worksheet: Philistine armor 42
Bible verse puzzle: How big was Goliath? 43

Worksheet: The mighty Goliath..44
Worksheet: Who was Goliath?..45

Lesson Four: David fights Goliath **46**
Bible word search puzzle: Defeating the giant..48
Coloring page: David fights Goliath..49
Worksheet: Who were the Philistines?..50
Bible word scramble: How did David defeat Goliath?..51
Worksheet: Facing the giant...52
Worksheet: Valley of Elah...53
Bible craft: Goliath's giant steps...54
Bible crossword puzzle: David defeats the Philistine..55
Worksheet: David and Goliath..56
Coloring worksheet: David defeats Goliath...57
Let's learn Hebrew: King Saul..58

Lesson Five: Israel celebrates! **60**
Coloring page: Israel celebrates...62
Bible quiz: Israel celebrates..63
Newspaper worksheet: Shepherd defeats giant!...64
Worksheet: Heroes and villains..65
Fill in the Blanks: Run away!..66
Worksheet: David and Jonathan...67
Worksheets: King of the Israelites..68
Worksheet: Who was David?..70
Creative writing: The day I defeated Goliath...71
Craft activity: Celebrate David's victory over Goliath...72
Let's learn Hebrew: Yehudah...74
Bible story activity: Write your own story of David & Goliath....................................76

Bible story cards: The story of David & Goliath..80

Crafts & Projects
Bible activity: Samuel anoints David..87
Bible craft: Make your own lyre..89
Worksheet: Who said it?...93
Bible craft: Make a slingshot..95

Answer Key 99
Discover more Activity Books!...104

LESSON ONE

David is anointed king: 1 Samuel 15:1-35 and 16:1-13

1. Lesson objectives:

During this lesson, children will explore:
1. Why God wanted a new king of Israel
2. How God chose the next king of Israel

2. Introduction:

To begin the lesson, ask your students to think about a time when they had to choose between doing what was right and taking the easy way out. Invite a few students to share their experiences. Explain that today's lesson is about a king named Saul who faced a similar choice. As a result of his decision, a young shepherd named David was chosen by God for a special task. Say, "What do you think happened after Saul disobeyed God? Let's find out!"

3. Review key vocabulary:

- **DAVID:** A young shepherd boy chosen by God to be the next king of Israel

- **SHEPHERD:** A person who takes care of sheep

- **ANOINT:** To pour oil on someone's head as a sign that God has chosen them for a special purpose

- **SAMUEL:** A prophet who listened to God and anointed the kings of Israel

- **AMALEKITES:** A group of people who lived in the time of the Bible and were enemies of Israel

4. Bible memory verse to help children remember God's Word:

"For God sees not as man sees: man looks on the outward appearance, but God looks at the heart." (1 Samuel 16:7)

5. Read 1 Samuel 15:1-35 and 16:1-13 or read the Bible story below:

In ancient Israel, there was a king named Saul. God told Saul to destroy everything in the Amalekite city because they were wicked. Saul gathered his army and attacked the city, but he did not fully obey God's command. He kept the best animals and spared the Amalekite king. When Samuel, the prophet, learned this, he was very upset. God told Samuel that He was sad He made Saul king because Saul had not obeyed Him. Samuel told Saul, "To obey is better than sacrifice." Because of Saul's disobedience, God decided to choose a new king of Israel. He sent Samuel to the house of Jesse in Bethlehem. Jesse had many sons, and Samuel was to anoint one of them as the next king. When Samuel saw Jesse's oldest son, he thought this must be the one God chose. But God said, "Do not look at his appearance. Man looks at the outside, but I look at the heart." Jesse presented seven of his sons, but God did not choose any of them. Samuel asked if there were any more sons. Jesse replied, "There is still the youngest, David, but he is tending the sheep." When David arrived, God told Samuel, "This is the one." Samuel anointed David as the next king of Israel, and the Spirit of God was with him.

6. Let's review:

1. What was today's story about?
2. What did God command King Saul to do to the Amalekite city?
3. Did King Saul fully obey God's command? What did he do instead?
4. How did Samuel feel when he learned that Saul did not fully obey God?
5. What did God do because Saul disobeyed Him?
6. Where did God send Samuel to find the next king of Israel?
7. Why did God choose David instead of Jesse's older sons?
8. What happened to David after Samuel anointed him as the next king of Israel?

7. Activites:

* Coloring page: Saul spares King Agag
* Worksheet: Who were the Amalekites?
* Worksheet: Saul spares King Agag
* Bible quiz: The prophet Samuel
* Worksheet: The prophet Samuel
* Worksheet: David the shepherd
* Bible activity: Samuel anoints David
* Newspaper worksheet: David anointed king!
* Worksheet: David is chosen king
* Worksheet: Discovering Bethlehem
* Worksheet: Jesse's family

"Saul... spared Agag and the best of the sheep and oxen..."

(1 Samuel 15:9)

Who were the Amalekites?

The Amalekites were a tribe of nomads who traveled on camels and lived in the deserts of Canaan, often on the outskirts of towns and villages. They lived in tents, usually made from black or brown wool and goat's hair, sewn together to provide a roof and sides. The open sides faced away from the wind, and the interior was usually separated by curtains into three sections: the men's section, the family section, and the kitchen. The floor was covered with rugs, and the owner's sword hung from the tent pole in the men's section. The tents had to be easy to set up and take down, light and portable, easy to repair, airy, and provide protection from the sun and cold.

Because of their nomadic lifestyle and their dislike of the Hebrew people, the Amalekites frequently attacked the Israelites. After Joshua conquered Canaan and divided it among the twelve tribes of Israel, God sent King Saul to wipe out an Amalekite city (likely a camp). Despite God's instructions to destroy everything, Saul kept the best animals and took the king of the Amalekites as his prisoner.

Read 1 Samuel 15:1-35 and the article above. Answer the questions.

1. How did the Amalekites live and travel in the deserts of Canaan?

   ....

   ....

2. What did King Saul do when God told him to destroy an Amalekite camp?

   ....

   ....

Saul spares King Agag

God asked King Saul to destroy the Amalekites. Did King Saul obey Him?
Read 1 Samuel 15:1-35, and write God's instructions to King Saul below.

Answer the questions below.

Why did God tell Saul to destroy the Amalekites?

How did King Saul's actions differ from God's instructions?

Why did Saul tell the Kenites to leave the Amalekites before the attack?

The prophet SAMUEL

Read 1 Samuel 1:1-2:21, 3:1-10, 8:1-10:27, 28:1-25, and 1 Chronicles 6:22-40. Answer the questions below.

1. When Samuel was called by God as a child, who did he think was calling him?

2. What did Samuel's mother bring him each year?

3. Why did Samuel never cut his hair?

4. What did the Israelites demand from Samuel?

5. What did Samuel warn the Israelites a king would do?

6. Who did Samuel anoint as the first king of the Israelites?

7. Samuel was from which tribe of Israel?

8. What were the names of Samuel's two sons?

9. What were Samuel's jobs?

10. What did Samuel tell Saul when he rose from the grave?

Samuel

If the battle between Saul and King Agag was a book, the cover would look like this…

Imagine you are an Israelite living in Bethlehem. What would you say to Samuel when he visited the city?

....
....
....
....
....
....
....
....
....

Describe King Saul's character.

....
....
....
....
....

Draw a picture of Samuel arriving in Bethlehem.

David the shepherd

Read 1 Chronicles 2:13–2:16, 1 Samuel 16:1-13 and 17:12-14. Complete the worksheet below.

Hometown:

....

David is most famous for:

....

David's older brothers were named:

....

....

Why do you think God chose David as king of Israel?

....

Draw a picture of Samuel anointing David as the next king of Israel.

The Bethlehem Times

City of Bethlehem

1 SAMUEL 16 — LAND OF ISRAEL — A BIBLE HISTORY PUBLICATION

Samuel visits city

....

....

....

....

....

....

Sheep for sale

David anointed king!

....

....

....

....

David is chosen king

Read 1 Samuel 16:7-13 (ESV). Using the words below, fill in the blanks to complete the Bible passage.

| HEART | SAMUEL | JESSE | SHAMMAH | ANOINT |
| BROTHERS | YOUNGEST | SHEEP | APPEARANCE | DAVID |

" God said to Samuel, "Do not look at his .... or at his physical stature, because I have refused him. For God does not see as man sees. Man looks at the outward appearance but I look at the ...." So, Jesse called Abinadab and made him pass before Samuel. And he said, "Neither has Yahweh chosen this one." Then Jesse made .... pass by. And he said, "Neither has God chosen this one." Jesse made seven of his sons pass before Samuel. And Samuel said to ...., "God has not chosen these." And Samuel said to Jesse, "Are all the young men here?" Then he said, "There is still the ...., and he is keeping the ...." Samuel said to Jesse, "Bring him here. For we will not sit down till he comes here." So, he sent and brought David in. Now he was ruddy, with bright eyes and good-looking. And God said, "Arise, ... him; for this is the one!" Then .... took the horn of oil and anointed .... in the midst of his .... And the Spirit of God came upon David from that day forward. "

Discovering Bethlehem

Bethlehem, a small town in Judah, holds significant importance in the Bible. It is first mentioned as the burial place of Rachel, Jacob's wife (Genesis 35:19). But it is best known as the hometown of David, Israel's greatest king, who was anointed by Samuel there (1 Samuel 16:1-13). Bethlehem was also prophesied as the birthplace of the Messiah, fulfilled in the New Testament with the birth of Yeshua the Messiah (Micah 5:2; Matthew 2:1-6).

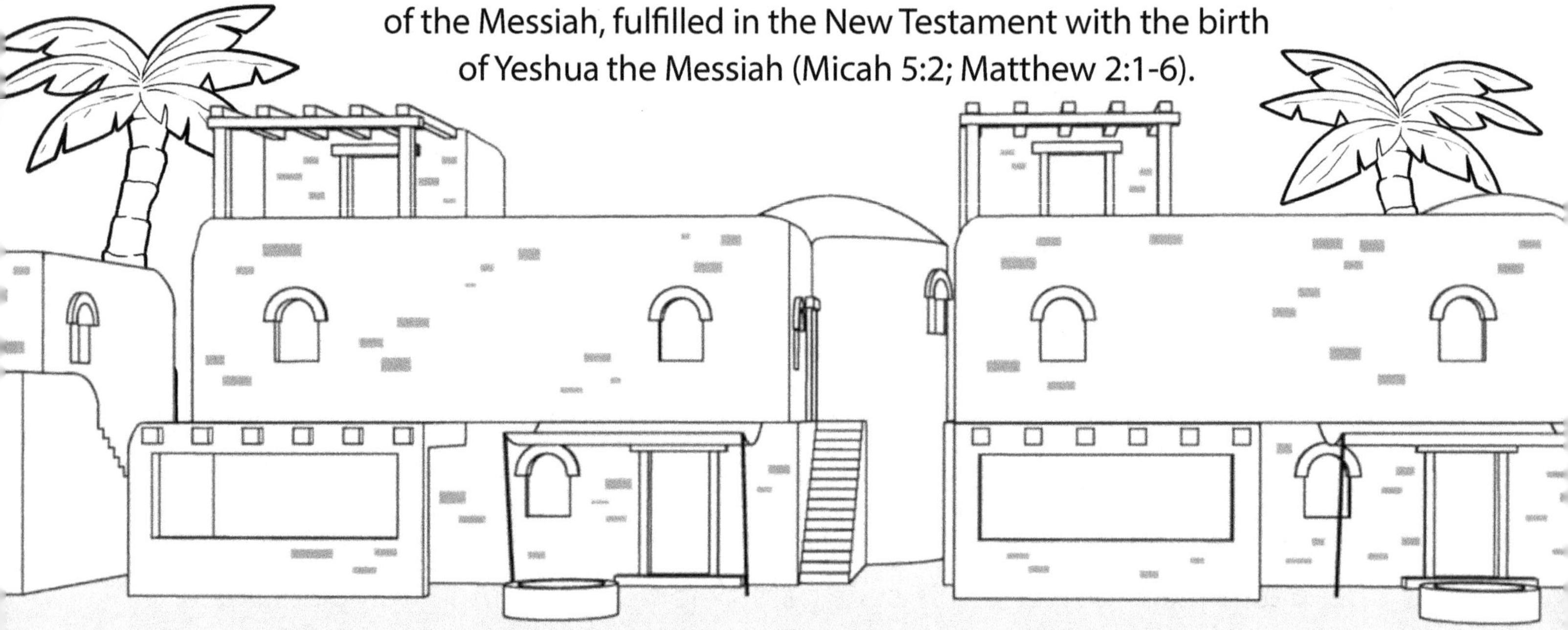

What famous events took place in Bethlehem? Read Genesis 48, Ruth 1, 1 Samuel 16, and Matthew 2. Answer the questions below.

Who did Jacob bury near Bethlehem?

....

Which two women returned to Bethlehem?

....

Who did Samuel find in Bethlehem?

....

Who ordered male babies in Bethlehem under two years old to be killed?

....

Jesse's family

Read 1 Chronicles 2:13–2:16 and 1 Samuel 17:12.
Write the names of Jesse's eight sons and two daughters in the boxes below.

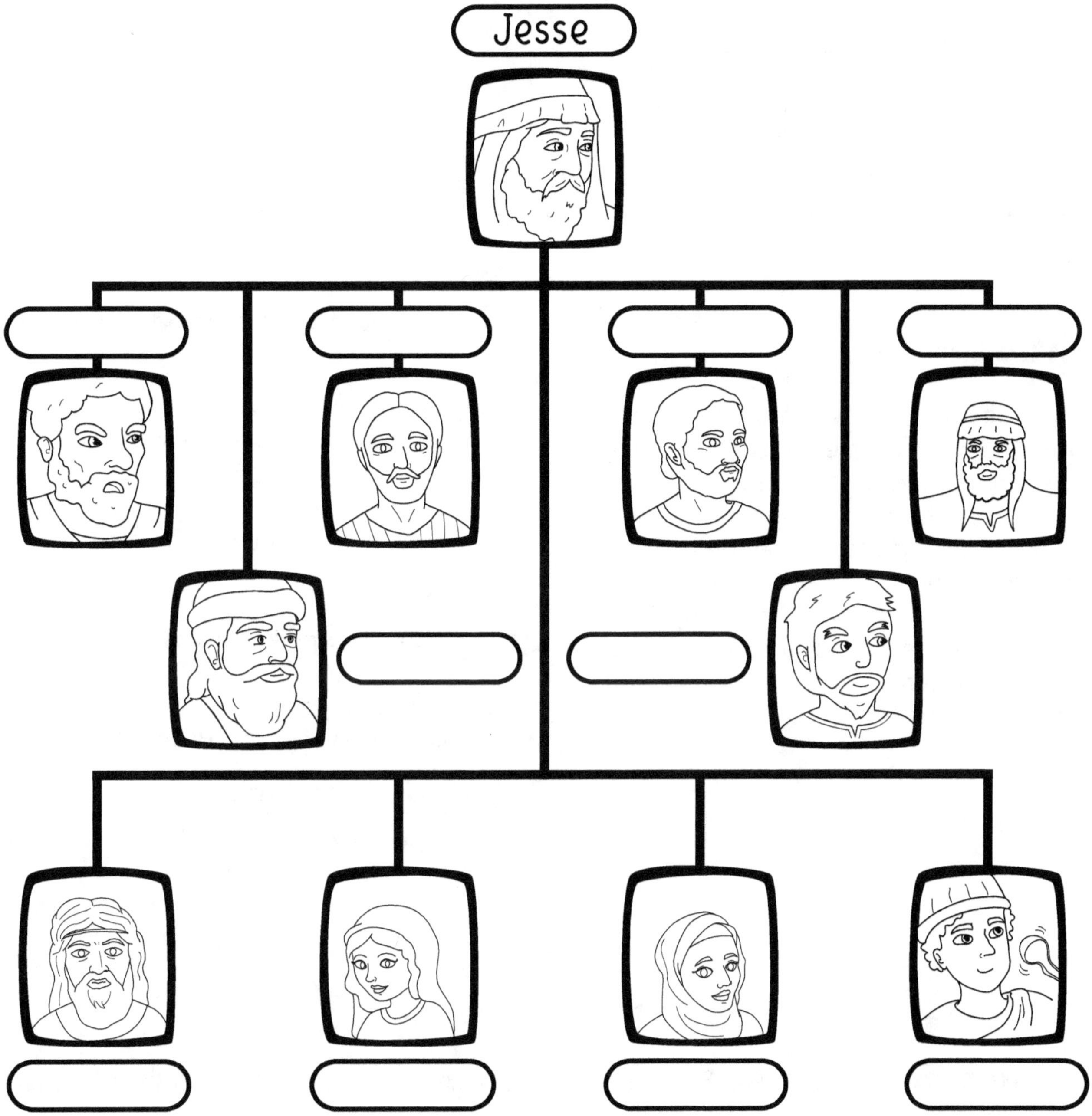

LESSON TWO

David works for King Saul: 1 Samuel 16:14-23

1. Lesson objectives:

During this lesson, children will explore:
1. How King Saul learned about David the shepherd
2. How David helped King Saul to overcome his torment

2. Introduction:

To begin the lesson, ask your students to think about a time when they felt sad or scared. Say, "What made you feel better during that time? Was it a song, a story, or maybe a hug from someone special?" Invite a few students to share their experiences. Then explain, "Today's lesson is about David, who helped King Saul feel better when he was troubled. David used a special talent to calm the king. What do you think that was? Let's find out!"

3. Review key vocabulary:

- **TORMENTED:** To be troubled or distressed
- **SKILLFUL:** Very good at doing something
- **LYRE:** A small harp-like musical instrument
- **VALOR:** Great bravery or courage
- **ARMOR-BEARER:** A person who carries the armor and weapons for a warrior or king

4. Bible memory verse to help children remember God's Word:

"Whenever the harmful spirit from God was upon Saul, David took the lyre and played it with his hand…" (1 Samuel 16:23)

5. Read 1 Samuel 16:14-23 or read the Bible story below:

One day, the Spirit of God left King Saul, and he began to feel very troubled by a harmful spirit. His servants noticed this and said to him, "A harmful spirit from God is bothering you. Let us find someone who can play the lyre (a small harp) well. When he plays, it will make you feel better." Saul agreed and told his servants to find someone who could play the lyre well and bring him to the palace. One of the young men said, "I know a son of Jesse from Bethlehem. His name is David. He is very good at playing the lyre, he is brave, a warrior, wise in speech, and he has a good presence. Most importantly, God is with him." So, Saul sent messengers to Jesse and said, "Send me your son David, who is with the sheep." Jesse took a donkey, loaded it with bread, a skin of wine, and a young goat, and sent them with David to King Saul. When David arrived, he entered Saul's service, and Saul loved him greatly. David became Saul's armor-bearer. Saul sent a message to Jesse saying, "Let David stay in my service, for he has found favor in my sight." Whenever the harmful spirit troubled Saul, David would take his lyre and play it. The music made Saul feel refreshed and well, and the harmful spirit would leave him.

6. Let's review:

1. What was today's story about?
2. What happened to King Saul when the Spirit of God left him?
3. What did Saul's servants suggest to help him feel better?
4. Who did one of the young men suggest to play the lyre for Saul?
5. What did Jesse send with David to King Saul?
6. What role did David take on when he arrived at Saul's palace?
7. How did Saul feel about David when he began to serve him?
8. What happened to Saul whenever David played the lyre for him?

7. Activites:

* Bible word search puzzle: David works for King Saul
* Worksheet: What did the Israelites wear?
* Maze activity: Help David visit King Saul
* Creative writing: David's hardworking helper
* Let's learn Hebrew: David
* Worksheet: Who was King Saul?
* Coloring page: David plays the lyre
* Map activity: Tribe of Benjamin
* Worksheet: David plays the lyre
* Worksheet: David and his lyre
* Creative writing: King Saul
* Bible craft: Make your own lyre

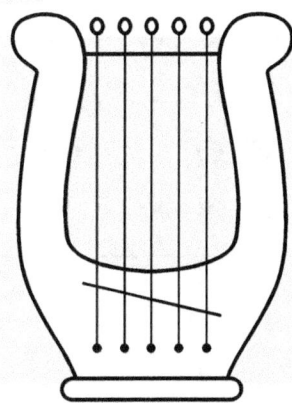

David works for KING SAUL

Read 1 Samuel 16:14-23. Find and circle the words below.

```
S A E L T V U S P I R I T E Z
X E H J R U O J A Y B M H F L
Y W R P I A U B L R U L W A O
A M K V L X W A O N R A T V J
C N R R I M T C B A Z K O O W
F X G W F C R M V J K F R R X
K D K S S S E D D W J E M D E
I M E S S E N G E R S J E A K
N H J M X D B M H A N E N V Y
G S L Y R E J W W X M S T I N
S R Y O U J F O C E J S E D A
A N E M K W J C I B L E D I C
U D A S E R V A N T S F B S X
L A R M O R - B E A R E R T B
G U D O N K E Y M A A W A V G
```

JESSE

DAVID

FAVOR

SPIRIT

SERVANTS

TORMENTED

LYRE

KING SAUL

DONKEY

SERVICE

ARMOR-BEARER

MESSENGERS

What did the Israelites wear?

During Bible times, Israelite men wore different clothes than men wear today. Most men wore an inner tunic, an outer robe or cloak, tzitzits, and sandals. Tunics were made from wool, linen, or cotton, and were held together at the waist by a belt made of leather or cloth. Outer robes were made of woolen cloth. Blue and white tzitzits made of linen or wool strands were worn to remind men to obey God's commandments (Numbers 15:37-41). Sandals were made of leather and dry grass, and had strings or ropes made of cheap materials. David, who was a shepherd before becoming King Saul's servant, would have worn similar clothing while tending his sheep. Using the Internet, your Bible, or an encyclopedia, research what men wore in Bible times. Write two facts about each item of clothing in the boxes below.

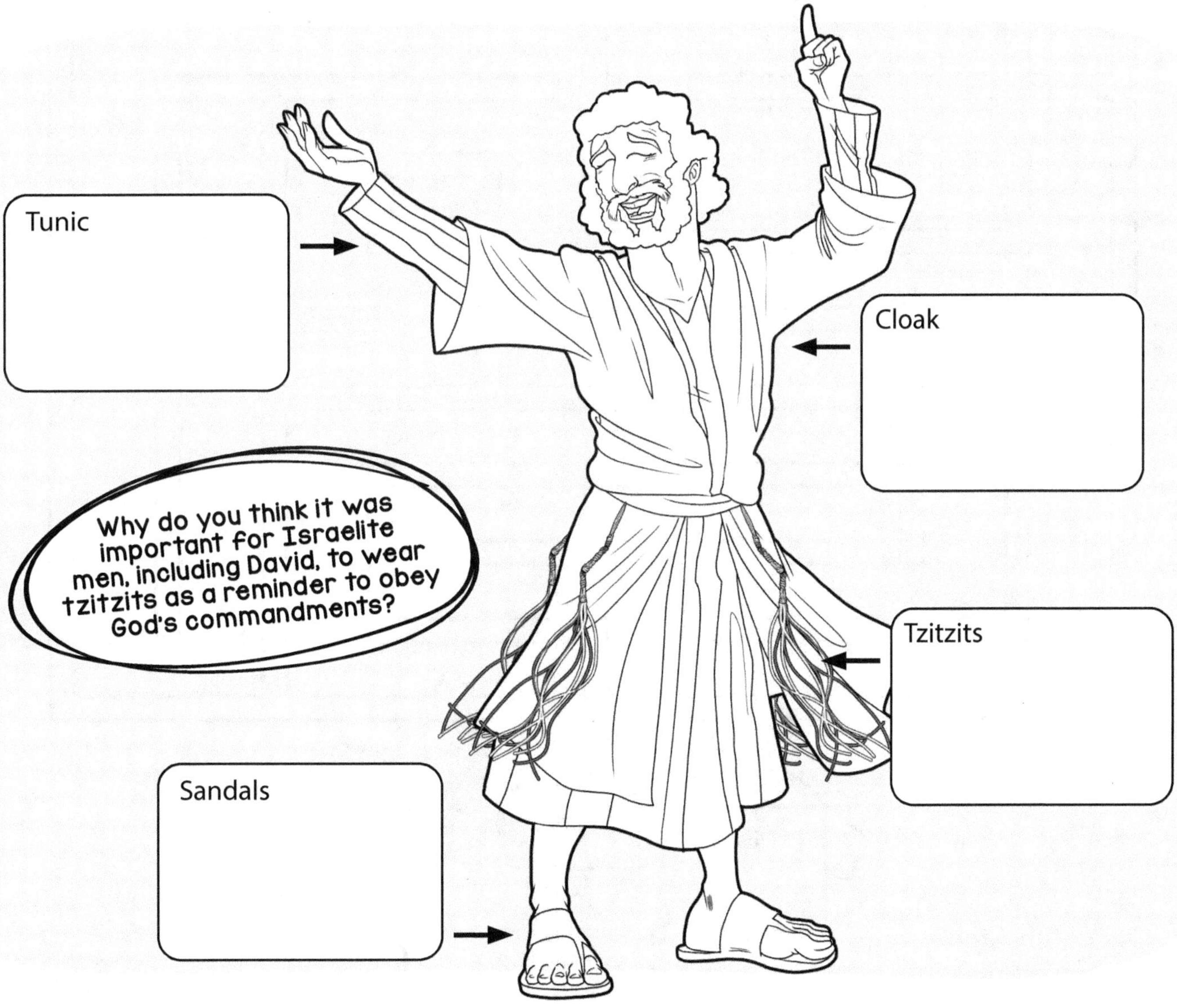

Tunic

Cloak

Why do you think it was important for Israelite men, including David, to wear tzitzits as a reminder to obey God's commandments?

Tzitzits

Sandals

David visits King Saul

Help David and his donkey find their way to King Saul's palace.

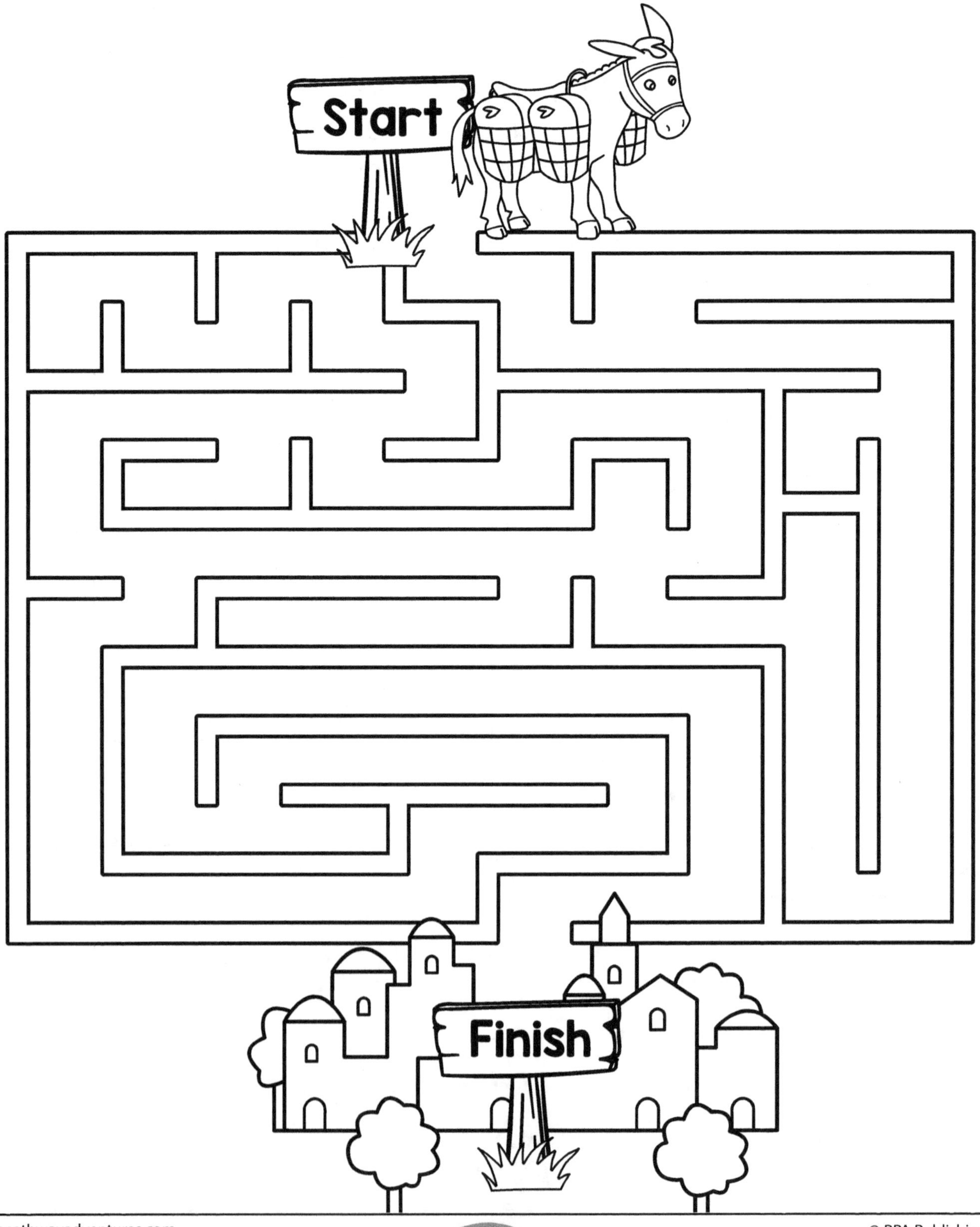

David's hardworking helper

In Bible times, donkeys were very important animals. They were used for many different tasks, such as carrying heavy loads, transporting people, and helping farmers with their work. Donkeys were strong and could travel long distances, making them valuable for journeys. In the Bible, we read stories about donkeys, like when Balaam's donkey spoke to him, when David took his donkey to visit King Saul, and when Yeshua rode a donkey into Jerusalem. Donkeys played a special role in people's lives and in many Bible stories, showing how useful and trusted they were.

Imagine you are David's donkey in Bible times. Write about the day you visited King Saul. Mention your role, the journey to Gibeah, and the people you met.

David

The Hebrew name for David is David (pronounced Da-VEED). Before David worked for King Saul, he lived in Bethlehem and worked as a shepherd. David became king of the Israelites when he was 30 years old. He was a great warrior who won many battles and even killed the giant Goliath with just a stone from his sling! King David wanted to build a temple, but God gave this job to his son, Solomon. David was from the tribe of Judah.

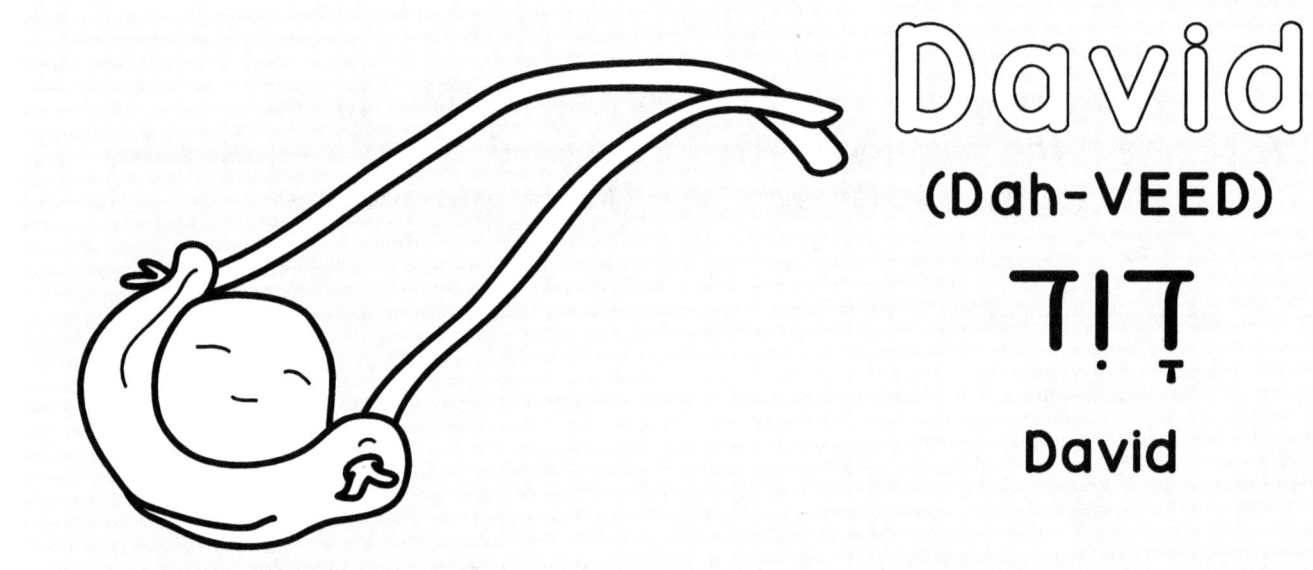

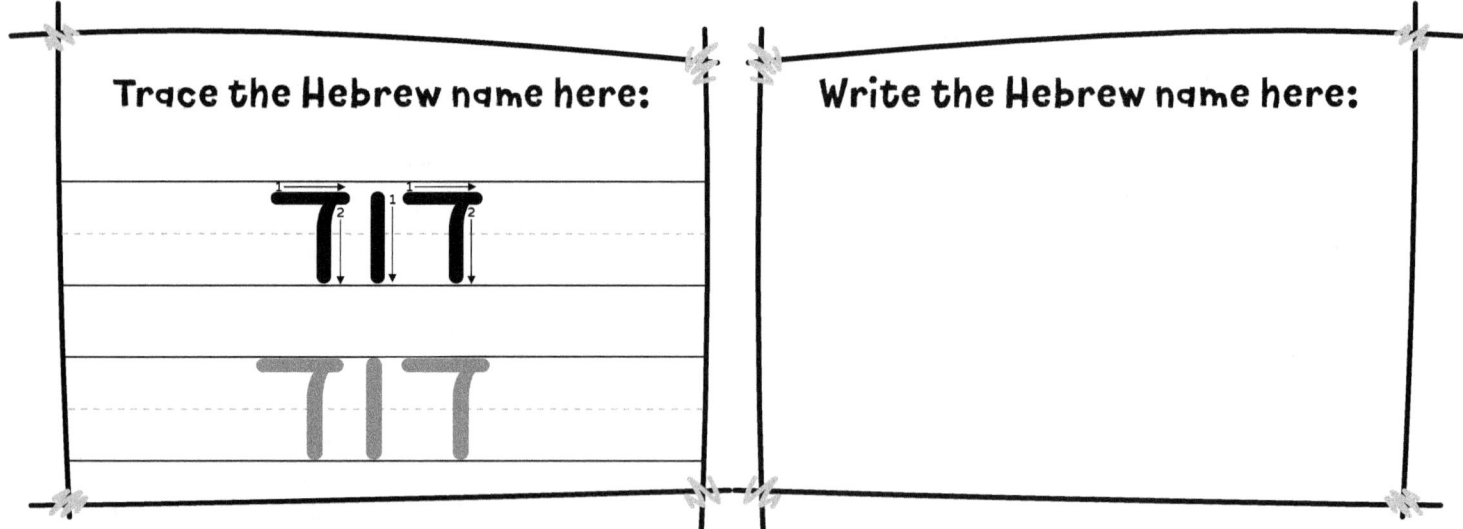

Let's write!

Write the Hebrew name 'David' on the lines below.

דוד

דוד

Try this on your own.
Remember that Hebrew is read from RIGHT to LEFT.

Who was King Saul?

Read 1 Samuel 10, 13:8-14, 15:1-23, 16:1-23, 18-19, 31, and the article below. Answer the questions.

Saul was from the tribe of Benjamin, one of the 12 tribes of Israel. He came from the village of Gibeah and became Israel's first king. His kingdom was not very big; it only included the area of Benjamin and the central highlands of Israel. King Saul set up his base in Gibeah, created a royal administration, and formed an army. Although Saul's kingdom wasn't large, it set the stage for future success under King David. Early in his reign, Saul's army defeated several enemies like the Ammonites, Moabites, Edomites, and Amalekites. However, God soon became unhappy with Saul. Saul disobeyed God by not completely destroying everything in a battle with the Amalekites, sparing their king and the best animals.

The word of God came to Samuel: "I regret that I have made Saul king, for he has turned back from following me and has not performed my commandments." (1 Samuel 15:10-11)

God decided to choose David, the youngest son of Jesse, to be the next king of Israel. Saul became jealous of David and tried to kill him many times. Even though Saul was angry with him, David stayed loyal and played the lyre to calm Saul when he was troubled. Despite Saul's efforts, David managed to escape each time. After Saul died in a battle against the Philistines, David became king and expanded the kingdom, bringing peace and prosperity to Israel.

1. How did David help calm King Saul when he was troubled?
   ....
   ....

2. Why did King Saul become jealous of David, and what did he try to do because of his jealousy?
   ....
   ....

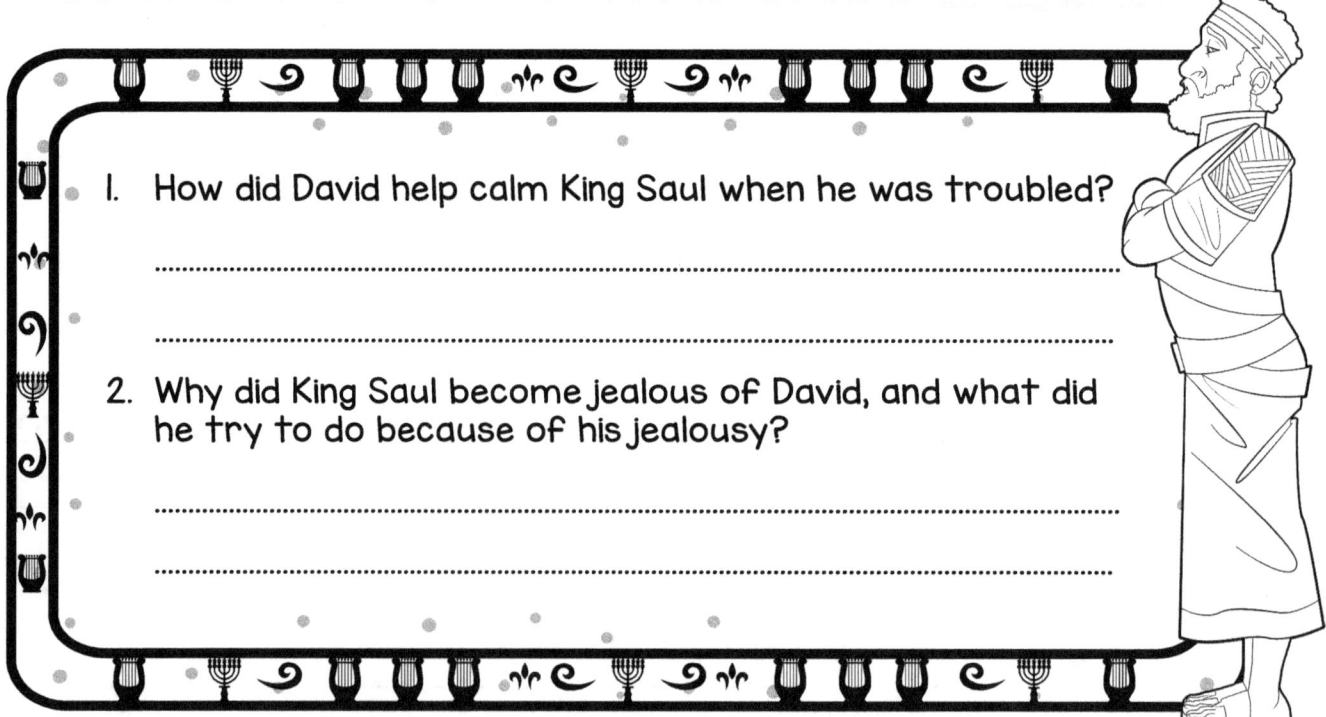

"**Whenever the harmful spirit from God was upon Saul, David took the lyre and played it with his hand.**"

(1 Samuel 16:23)

Tribe of Benjamin

King Saul was from the tribe of Benjamin, one of the 12 tribes of Israel. When the Israelites took over the land of Canaan, each tribe was given a piece of this land. The tribe of Benjamin received a region described in the Book of Joshua (Joshua 18:11-28). Their land stretched from the Jordan River in the east, near the Dead Sea, to the city of Bethel in the northwest and Jerusalem in the south. Although the territory of Benjamin was small, it was located between two important areas: Ephraim to the north and Judah to the south. The tribe of Benjamin's location, with access to the Jordan River and the Dead Sea, allowed for lots of trade. The eastern part of their land was good for farming, and the mountains in the middle of their territory provided protection from enemies.

Read Joshua 18:11-28 and 1 Samuel 9-10, 13-15. Answer the questions. Color the map.

1. What advantages did the tribe of Benjamin have because of their location in Israel?

   ....

2. Why was the territory of the tribe of Benjamin important despite its small size?

   ....

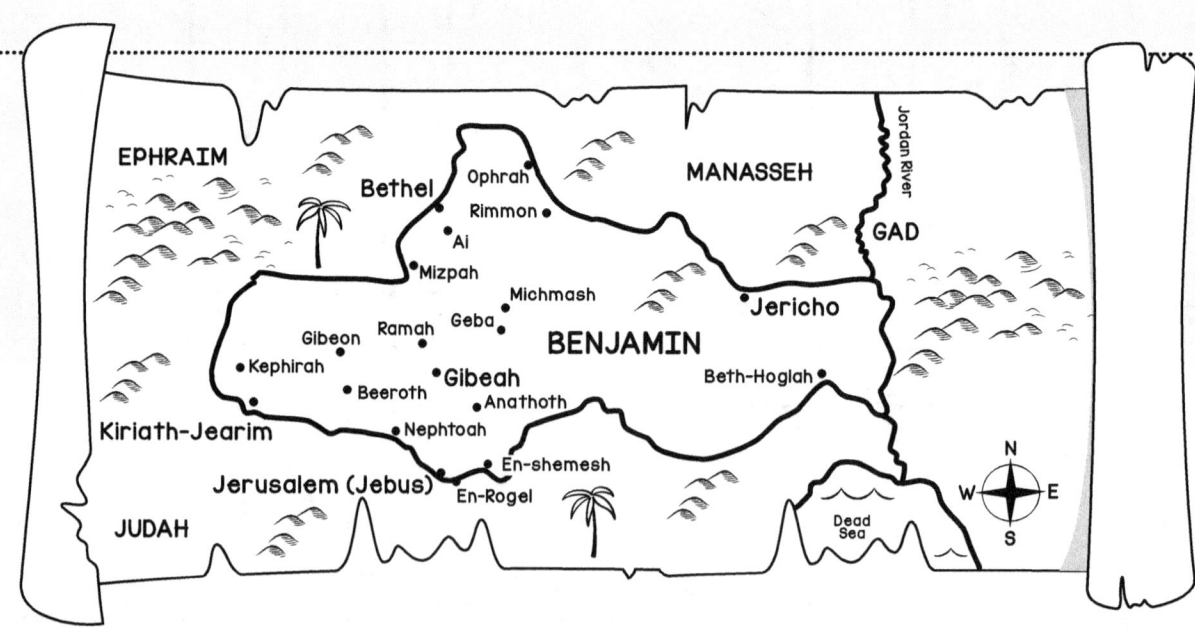

David plays the lyre

How did King Saul's servant describe David?
Read 1 Samuel 16:14-23, and write this description below.

Answer the questions below.

| Why did Saul's servants suggest finding someone who could play the lyre? | Who did one of Saul's servants recommend to play the lyre for Saul, and why? | What happened when David played the lyre for Saul? |

David and his lyre

A lyre is a musical instrument that looks like a small harp. It has a U-shaped frame with two arms connected by a crossbar. The strings, usually made of gut or nylon, are stretched between the crossbar and the base of the instrument. The number of strings can vary, but most lyres have between 7 to 10 strings. The sound of a lyre is gentle and soothing, similar to a soft harp or guitar. In the Bible, David played the lyre. When King Saul was troubled by an evil spirit, David would play the lyre to help him feel better. The beautiful music from the lyre would bring relief to Saul (1 Samuel 16:23).

Draw a picture of a lyre in the space below.

Color young David playing the lyre.

Read 1 Samuel 15:1-16:23. Imagine yourself as King Saul.

Write a short paragraph describing a day in the life of a king of Israel, and how young David helped you.

....

....

....

....

....

....

....

LESSON THREE

Facing Goliath: 1 Samuel 17:1-16

1. Lesson objectives:

During this lesson, children will explore:
1. Where the Philistines and Israelites gathered for battle
2. Why the Israelites were afraid to fight Goliath

2. Introduction:

Before the class begins, get a sheet of wrapping paper long enough to represent the height of a giant (Goliath was approximately 9.5 feet tall). Mount the sheet on the classroom wall. As your students arrive, ask each one to stand in front of the sheet to be measured. Make marks over their heads and write their names next to these marks. Say, "Have you ever seen a person as tall as this sheet of paper?" Then, explain that today's lesson focuses on an enemy giant named Goliath. Say, "What do you think the Israelites thought when they faced a giant like Goliath on the battlefield? Let's find out!"

3. Review key vocabulary:

- **PHILISTINES:** A group of people who lived near the Israelites and often fought with them
- **GOLIATH:** A Philistine giant
- **SHIELD-BEARER:** A man who carried a shield to protect a soldier during battle
- **ARMOR:** A special suit made of metal or other strong materials that Goliath wore to protect himself during battle
- **BRONZE:** A type of metal that is a mixture of copper and tin

4. Bible memory verse to help children remember God's Word:

"There came out from the camp of the Philistines a champion named Goliath of Gath, whose height was six cubits and a span." (1 Samuel 17:4)

5. Read 1 Samuel 17:1-16 or read the Bible story below:

The Philistines gathered their armies for battle at a place called Socoh, in Judah. King Saul and the men of Israel camped in the Valley of Elah, with the Philistines on one mountain and Israel on another, separated by a valley. A giant named Goliath came out from the Philistine camp. He was incredibly tall and wore heavy bronze armor. He carried a huge spear and had a shield-bearer in front of him. Goliath shouted to the Israelites, "Why have you come out to fight? I am a Philistine, and you are servants of Saul. Choose a man to fight me. If he can kill me, we will be your servants. But if I kill him, you will be our servants." Goliath continued, "I defy the ranks of Israel today. Give me a man to fight!" When King Saul and the Israelites heard this, they were very afraid. David, the youngest son of Jesse from Bethlehem, was taking care of his father's sheep. Jesse had eight sons, and the three oldest were with Saul at the battle. Every day, for forty days, Goliath came forward and challenged the Israelites, but no one dared to fight him. David went back and forth from Saul to tend to his father's sheep, unaware that soon he would face the giant and change the course of the battle.

6. Let's review:

1. What was today's story about?
2. Where did the Philistines and Israelites gather for battle?
3. Who was the giant warrior that came out from the Philistine camp?
4. What kind of armor and weapons did Goliath have?
5. What challenge did Goliath give to the Israelites?
6. How did King Saul and the Israelites feel when they heard Goliath's challenge?
7. How long did Goliath come out and challenge the Israelites?
8. Who was David, and what was he doing during this time?

7. Activites:

* Bible quiz: Facing Goliath
* Coloring page: Goliath
* Worksheets: The Nephilim
* Worksheet: Match the scriptures
* Map activity: Valley of Elah
* Worksheet: Valley of Elah
* Worksheet: How big was Goliath?
* Worksheet: Who said it?
* Worksheet: Philistine armor
* Bible verse puzzle: How big was Goliath?
* Worksheet: The mighty Goliath
* Worksheet: Who was Goliath?

Facing GOLIATH

Read 1 Samuel 15-17. Answer the questions below.

1. In which Philistine town did Goliath live?

2. How long did Goliath challenge the Israelites to a fight?

3. Why did the Israelite army fear Goliath?

4. What metal was Goliath's armor made from?

5. How tall was Goliath?

6. Who challenged Goliath to a fight?

7. How heavy was Goliath's armor plate?

8. How did David kill Goliath?

9. In which valley did the Philistine and Israelite soldiers face each other?

10. Where in the Bible do we read about Goliath?

"Choose one man and send him to fight me."

(1 Samuel 17:8)

The Nephilim

This article looks at discoveries around the world that appear to prove the existence of giants. As you read it, think about the Israelite soldiers who faced Goliath on the battlefield. Then, answer the questions on the next page.

Who were the giants?

According to the Bible and ancient legends, there was a race of giants and superheroes known as the Nephilim who did acts of great evil. They were physical beings produced by the union of fallen angels and human women (Genesis 6:1-4).

The Nephilim were huge! Ancient records and skeletons found worldwide show they were up to 20 feet tall. For example, a skeleton found in 1692 in a tomb near Angers, France, measured seventeen feet tall. In 1833, soldiers digging a pit at Lompock Rancho, California, unearthed a twelve-foot giant with a double row of teeth. Around 1950, tombs containing giants fourteen to sixteen feet tall were discovered in the Euphrates Valley of southeastern Turkey. In 2014, on Mount Shoria in southern Siberia, researchers found a massive wall of granite stones stacked 40 meters high. Some of these stones were estimated to weigh more than 3,000 tons, and many of them had flat surfaces, right angles, and sharp corners. Who built these large structures?

The Nephilim were more than simply big; they were also violent and wicked. Some had physical characteristics that were different from humans, such as double rows of teeth and six fingers or toes on each hand or foot (2 Samuel 21:20). The most famous Nephilim of the Bible was Goliath of Gath.

The Nephilim

Who were the Nephilim?

What unusual physical characteristics did some Nephilim have that were different from humans?

How tall were some of the Nephilim according to ancient records and skeletons found around the world?

What famous Nephilim is mentioned in the Bible, and which group of soldiers faced him on the battlefield?

Match the scriptures

In 1 Samuel 17:1-16, the Israelites faced the Philistines, ready for battle. Match the Bible verse to the correct scripture to learn how these two camps prepared for battle.

"There came out from the camp of the Philistines a champion named Goliath of Gath, whose height was six cubits and a span." → 1 Samuel 17:16

"Why have you come out to draw up for battle? Am I not a Philistine, and are you not servants of Saul? Choose a man for yourselves, and let him come down to me." → 1 Samuel 17:4

"When Saul and all Israel heard these words of the Philistine, they were dismayed and greatly afraid." → 1 Samuel 17:11

"For forty days the Philistine came forward and took his stand, morning and evening." → 1 Samuel 17:8

Valley of Elah

The Philistines gathered their armies for battle at Sochoh, which belongs to Judah, and encamped between Sochoh and Azeka in Ephes-dammim. King Saul and the Israelites were gathered and encamped in the Valley of Elah, and drew up in line of battle against the Philistines (1 Samuel 17:1-3). Imagine you are an Israelite soldier. Write a short paragraph about how the Israelite camp felt when they saw Goliath. Then, draw the army camps on the map.

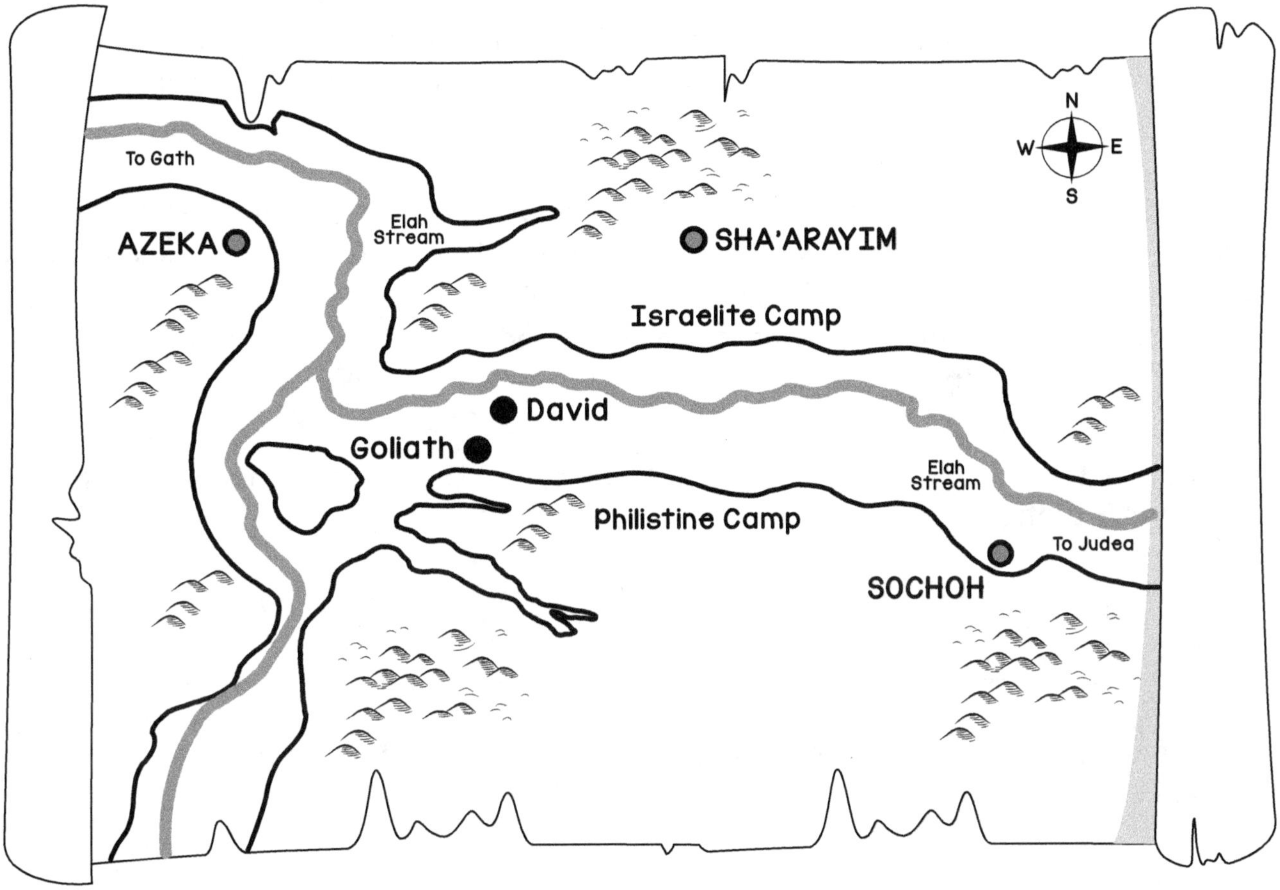

....

....

....

....

Valley of Elah

Read 1 Samuel 17 and the article below. Answer the questions.

The valley near Bethlehem where David and Goliath battled before the Philistine and Israelite armies was called the Valley of Elah. The Philistine army positioned themselves on the western slopes near Azekah, while King Saul and his army camped in the high country on the eastern side of the valley closer to Socoh. The valley formed the battle line between the two armies that were camped on opposite sides. Unlike modern armies, soldiers in biblical times had to provide their own food and help provide food for others. Jesse chose the right day to send David to the battlefield with food supplies for his three brothers.

Every day for forty days, Goliath challenged an Israelite soldier to fight him. This was an example of "representational combat." Two heroes fought on behalf of their respective armies, and the winner took victory for his tribe or nation. This system helped avoid lots of deaths on both sides. As leader of the Israelites, King Saul should have fought Goliath. Instead, it was David, the shepherd, who finally accepted Goliath's challenge.

1. Where did the Philistine and Israelite armies position themselves in the Valley of Elah?

   ....

   ....

2. What was "representational combat," and why was it used in battles like the one between David and Goliath?

   ....

   ....

3. Why do you think King Saul did not fight Goliath himself and instead allowed David to accept the challenge?

   ....

   ....

How big was Goliath?

How tall were David and Goliath? Using the Bible, the Internet, or an encyclopedia, research the height of Goliath and the ancient Israelites. Draw David and Goliath next to the yardstick to show their heights.

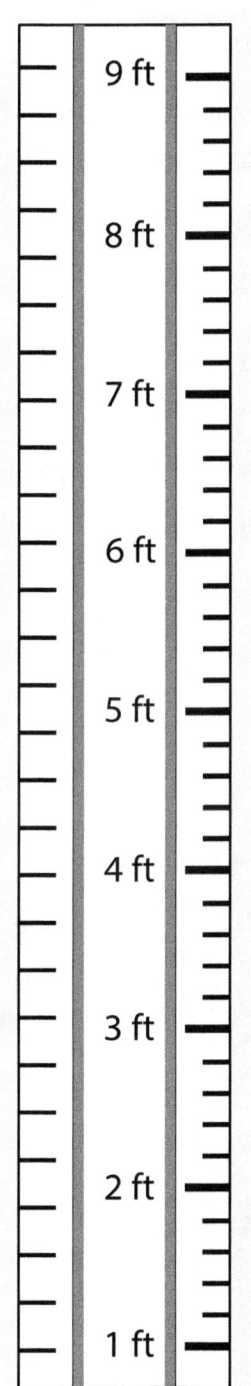

Philistine armor

The Philistines were an aggressive, warlike people who lived in southwest Palestine between the Mediterranean Sea and the Jordan River. For nearly 200 years, they were Israel's most dangerous enemy. They frequently attacked the Israelites and invaded their land, and their superior iron weapons made them hard to beat in battle. Philistine soldiers wore a "feather" headdress, a leather cap, and an ornamental headband with slightly curving strips that stood upright. These curving strips were made of feathers, reeds, leather strips, or horsehair, and were held in place by metal headbands. Their body armor included breastplates and skirts with wide hems and tassels. Soldiers sometimes carried small round shields and straight swords.

Design your own Philistine helmet in the space below. Use your imagination!

Color the Philistine soldier!

How big was Goliath!

This Bible verse is written in code. Use the chart at the bottom of the page to fill in the missing letters and crack the code! *Hint: Read 1 Samuel 17:4 (ESV)*

```
_  _  O  _  _  _  _  _  _  O  _  _  _  _  O  _  _  _  _
23 26 20 21 20 12 22 9 20  1  6 23 19 21  1  9 23 26 20

_  _  _  O  _  _  _  _  _  _  I  _  I  _  _  I  N  _  _
12 22 9  8  1 19 23 26 20  8 26 25 10 25 15 23 25  5 20 15

_  _  _  _  I  O  N  N  _  _  _  _  _  _  G  O  _  I  _  _  _  O  _
22 12 26 22 9  8 25  1  5  5 22  9 20  3 17  1 10 25 22 23 26  1 19

G  _  _  _  _  O  _  _  _  _  I  G  _  _  _  _  _  I  _
17 22 23 26  4 26  1 15 20 26 20 25 17 26 23  4 22 15 15 25 16

_  _  _  I  _  _   N  _  _   _  _  _  _  N.
12 6  7 25 23 15  22  5  3  22 15  8 22  5
```

A	B	C	D	E	F	G	H	I	J	K	L	M
						17		25				

N	O	P	Q	R	S	T	U	V	W	X	Y	Z
5	1											

The mighty Goliath

"There came out from the camp of the Philistines a champion named Goliath of Gath…" (1 Samuel 17:4) Now, imagine you are Goliath, the giant warrior from 1 Samuel 17. A magazine has sent you some questions. Answer the questions below as if you were Goliath. Think about how he might feel and what he might say.

1. Introduce yourself.

....
....

2. Why do you challenge just one Israelite to fight you?

....
....

3. What makes you so confident you can defeat any Israelite?

....
....

4. How do you prepare for battle during the 40 days of challenges?

....

Who was Goliath?

Read 1 Samuel 17. Complete the worksheet below.

Hometown:

....

Goliath was .... feet tall.

In battle, Goliath wore:

....

Goliath is most famous for:

....

....

....

....

Draw a picture of Goliath challenging an Israelite to fight him in the Valley of Elah:

LESSON FOUR

David fights Goliath: 1 Samuel 17:21-51

1. Lesson objectives:

During this lesson, children will explore:
1. How David prepared for battle
2. How David defeated Goliath

2. Introduction:

To begin the class, set the scene of an epic battle. Ask your students to imagine standing on a battlefield with two men, David and Goliath, facing each other. Bring a large measuring tape and stretch it out to show Goliath's height of about 9 feet. Next, present five small stones and a simple slingshot, explaining that young David chose these as his only weapons. Say, "What do you think happened when David finally faced Goliath on the battlefield with only a sling and five stones? Let's find out!"

3. Review key vocabulary:

- **JAVELIN:** A long spear that people throw in sports or in battle
- **ELIAB:** David's older brother
- **ARMOR:** A special suit made of metal or other strong materials
- **YAHWEH:** Another name for God
- **VALLEY OF ELAH:** A long, shallow valley in the land of Israel

4. Bible memory verse to help children remember God's Word:

"…You come to me with a sword, a spear and a javelin, but I come to you in the name of Yahweh, the God of the armies of Israel…" (1 Samuel 17:45)

5. Read 1 Samuel 17:21-51 or read the Bible story below:

The Philistines and Israelites were ready for battle. Goliath called out to the Israelites, "Why have a full battle? Choose someone to fight me. If I win, you serve us. If he wins, we'll serve you." Meanwhile, David visited his brothers on the battlefield. When he heard about Goliath's challenge, he asked, "Who is this man defying God's army? What do we get if we beat him?" King Saul learned of David's courage and sent for him. David told Saul, "No one should be afraid. I'll fight Goliath." Saul did not believe David could defeat Goliath, but David explained how he'd fought off lions and bears to protect his sheep and believed that God would help him against Goliath. So, David, with his staff, five stones, and a sling, went out to face Goliath. Goliath made fun of David, but David was not afraid. "You come against me with a sword, spear, and javelin. But I come in God's name, and He will deliver you into my hands." Goliath had heard enough. He raised his spear and stomped towards David. Clouds of dust rose with each step the giant made, but David wasn't afraid. He grabbed a stone from his bag, put it in his sling, and swung it above his head. *Whoosh! Whoosh! Whoosh!* David aimed at the giant and let it fly. The stone whizzed through the air like a rocket and smacked Goliath in the middle of his huge, hairy forehead. Goliath stumbled forward and crashed to the ground. The Philistines stared in astonishment. They couldn't believe a young shepherd had just defeated their mighty giant, Goliath!

6. Let's review:

1. What was today's story about?
2. Who were the two main characters facing each other in the battle?
3. How tall was Goliath?
4. What weapons did David choose to fight Goliath?
5. How did the Israelites feel when they saw Goliath?
6. What did Goliath say to David when he saw him?
7. How did David respond to Goliath's taunts?
8. What happened when David used his slingshot against Goliath?

7. Activites:

* Bible word search puzzle: Defeating the giant
* Coloring page: David fights Goliath
* Worksheet: Who were the Philistines?
* Bible word scramble: How did David defeat Goliath?
* Bible craft: Make a slingshot
* Worksheet: Facing the giant
* Worksheet: Valley of Elah
* Bible craft: Goliath's giant steps
* Bible crossword puzzle: David defeats the Philistine
* Worksheet: David and Goliath
* Coloring worksheet: David defeats Goliath
* Let's learn Hebrew: King Saul

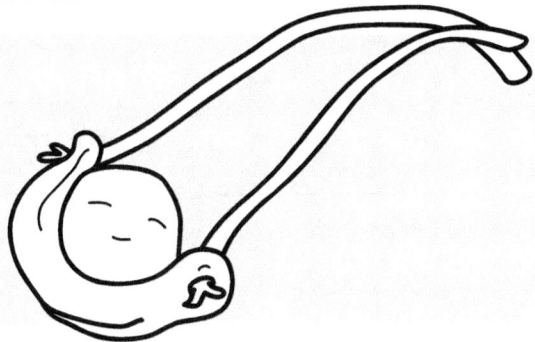

Defeating the GIANT

Read 1 Samuel 17:19-51. Find and circle the words below.

```
P B E Q Z Q Y I E I U P E M S
S T A F F Y U P G F K H Y X W
J B S T H S G S K H M I K A O
P U O A T N D M I U R L D R R
R G O B O L D K N C X I G M D
N W P V X W E P G X D S M I R
A J O M M D X Z S J Z T S E R
M E N O F I S R A E L I L S F
E Q L B C L T Y U J Q N I Y H
D R L Z M B W F L Y Q E N S W
T R V Q Y U D X N G T S G H P
Q S E R V A N T J J B M W Z I
A O G Z E F U Y F J L W D H G
L C S T O N E G A R M O R C U
H T P E Q G I A N T V U H Y S
```

GIANT
BATTLE
SLING
ARMIES
PHILISTINES
MEN OF ISRAEL
STONE
SWORD
STAFF
KING SAUL
SERVANT
ARMOR

"David ran quickly toward the battle line to meet Goliath..."

(1 Samuel 17:48)

Who were the Philistines?

It is believed that the Philistines originally came from the Aegean region, possibly from the island of Crete. They are thought to have migrated to the coast of Palestine around the 12th century BCE. They lived on the coastal plains of Palestine in five main cities: Gaza, Ashkelon, Ashdod, Gath, and Ekron. Until their defeat by King David, Philistine cities were ruled by a "king" or "lord." In times of trouble, these kings worked together to fight the Israelites. Judges 13–16 tells of Samson's many battles and encounters with the Philistines. Philistine cities contained fortresses, palaces, temples, markets, and even wineries. They were highly skilled in smithing iron, which gave them superior weapons. The Israelites were forced to go to the Philistines to get their own tools and weapons sharpened (1 Samuel 13:1-23).

The Philistines worshiped three gods: Astarte, Dagon, and Beelzebub. Artifacts found in the ruins of these cities show that the Philistine soldiers carried images of these gods into battle. Today, archaeologists have uncovered evidence that proves the Philistine culture was as advanced as their iron weapons. The word "philistine" is often used to describe an uncultured person. However, the Philistines were actually a very sophisticated people.

Read the article above. Answer the questions.

1. Where did the Philistines originally come from, and which five main cities did they inhabit?

....

....

2. Read 1 Samuel 13:1-23: Why did the Israelites go to the Philistines to get their weapons sharpened?

....

....

How did David defeat Goliath?

Unscramble the words to find the answer. *Hint: Read 1 Samuel 17:50 (ESV).*

"divDa dveieralp eovr teh

_____

Pihsitniel thwi a snlgi and

_____

hwit a otens..."

_____

Facing the giant

Read 1 Samuel 17:45-50. Using the words below, fill in the blanks to complete the Bible passage.

| FOREHEAD | GOLIATH | DELIVER | ARMIES | HEAD |
| SLING | ASSEMBLY | BATTLE | STONE | PHILISTINES |

" David said to ………………………, "You come to me with a sword and with a spear and with a javelin, but I come to you in the name of Yahweh, the God of the ………………………… of Israel, whom you have defied. This day God will ………………………… you into my hand, and I will strike you down and cut off your ………………………… I will give the dead bodies of the host of the ………………………… this day to the birds of the air and to the wild beasts of the earth, that all the earth may know that there is a God in Israel, and that all this ………………………… may know that God saves not with sword and spear. For the battle is God's, and He will give you into our hand." When Goliath arose and drew near to meet David, David ran quickly toward the ………………………… line to meet him. He put his hand in his bag and took out a ………………………… and slung it and struck the Philistine on his ………………………… The stone sank into his forehead, and he fell on his face to the ground. David prevailed over Goliath with a ………………………… and with a stone, and struck the Philistine and killed him. "

Valley of Elah

Draw a map of the Valley of Elah. Show the Philistine and Israelite armies.

Imagine you are an Israelite soldier. What would you say to David as he went out to face Goliath?
....
....
....
....
....
....
....

Describe David's character.
....
....
....
....
....
....

If the battle between David and Goliath was a book, the cover would look like this…

Goliath's giant steps

You will need:
1. Cardboard
2. Marker
3. Pipe cleaners

Instructions:

1. Draw a large foot onto a piece of cardboard and cut it out.
2. Turn it over and trace it onto another piece of cardboard, then cut it out. This way, you will get a matching left and right foot.
3. Cut four holes into each foot around where your child's foot will go. Thread the pipe cleaners through from the back (two pipe cleaners for each foot).
4. Place your child's feet onto the cardboard feet and fasten them with the pipe cleaners.

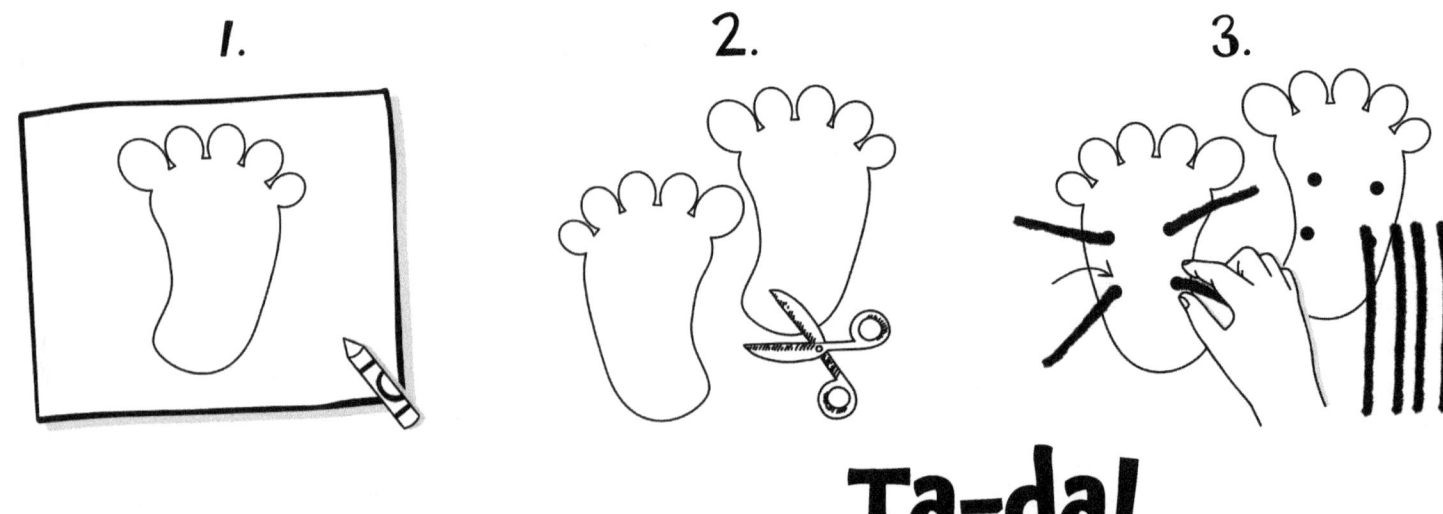

Ta-da!

David defeats the PHILISTINE

Read 1 Samuel 17:1-51 (ESV). Complete the crossword below.

ACROSS

3) The group of people Goliath belonged to.
5) David picked five of these from a stream.
6) The valley where the battle took place.
7) David struck Goliath on this part of his body.
9) David's older brothers were in this.

DOWN

1) The giant who fought David.
2) David used this weapon to defeat Goliath.
4) Goliath's height was six cubits and a ____.
5) The king of Israel during this battle.
8) The young shepherd who fought the giant.

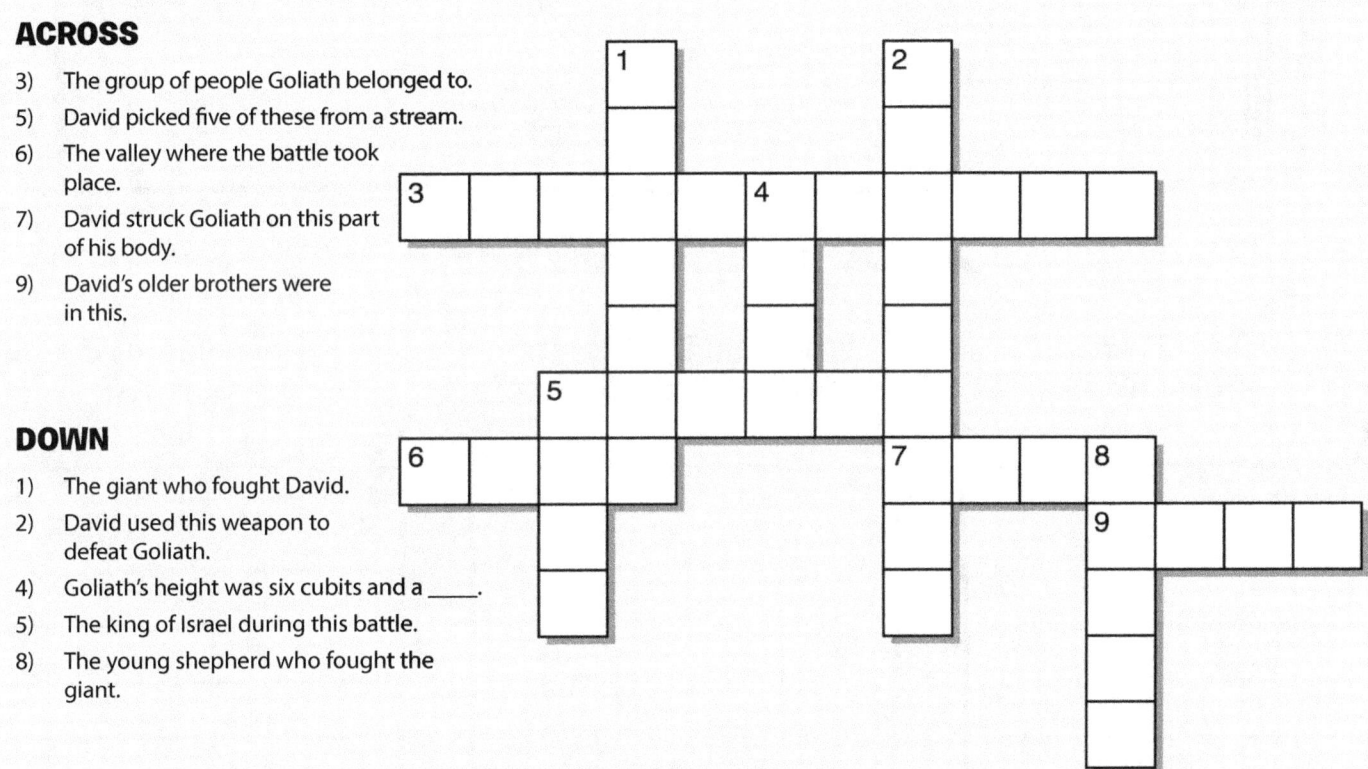

David and Goliath

David faced and defeated the giant Goliath. How did he do it?
Read 1 Samuel 17:21-51, then write a short summary of the story below.

Answer the questions below.

| How tall was Goliath? | What did David wear when he faced Goliath? | How did David kill Goliath? |

www.biblepathwayadventures.com
The story of David & Goliath Activity Book

© BPA Publishing Ltd 2024

David defeats Goliath

David and Goliath met on the battlefield in the Valley of Elah. Read 1 Samuel 17:41-51 and the story below. Then write David and Goliath's conversation in the speech bubbles below.

David said to King Saul. "Let no man's heart fail because of him. Your servant will go and fight this Philistine." Saul looked at the young shepherd with disbelief. "You are not able to go against this Philistine to fight with him, for you are but a youth, and he has been a man of war from his youth," Saul responded. But David was undeterred. He recounted his past experiences, saying, "Your servant used to keep sheep for his father. When a lion or a bear came and took a lamb, I went after it, struck it, and rescued the lamb. If the animal rose against me, I caught it by its beard, struck it, and killed it. This Philistine will be like one of them, for he has defied the armies of the living God. God who delivered me from the paw of the lion and the bear will deliver me from this Philistine." Seeing David's faith and courage, Saul finally said, "Go, and God be with you."

www.biblepathwayadventures.com
The story of David & Goliath Activity Book

© BPA Publishing Ltd 2024

King Saul

The Hebrew name for Saul is Sha'ul. Saul was the tallest man in Israel (1 Samuel 9:2). God chose him to be the first king of Israel. King Saul ruled the Israelites well for many years, but then he stopped listening to God and began to behave badly (1 Samuel 15:11). When David volunteered to fight Goliath, King Saul tried to give David his armor, but David refused it, saying he wasn't used to it (1 Samuel 17:38-39). Later, Saul did something very wrong by asking a medium to contact the prophet Samuel. God had had enough, and Saul was killed in battle the next day (1 Samuel 31:1-4).

Sha'ul
(Shah-OOL)

שָׁאוּל

Saul

Trace the Hebrew name here:

שָׁאוּל

שָׁאוּל

Write the Hebrew name here:

Let's write!

Practice writing Saul's Hebrew name on the lines below.

שאול

שאול

Try this on your own.
Remember that Hebrew is read from RIGHT to LEFT.

LESSON FIVE

Israel celebrates: 1 Samuel 17:50-18:7

1. Lesson objectives:

During this lesson, children will explore:
1. How the Israelites reacted to David's success in battle
2. How David and King Saul's son Jonathan became friends

2. Introduction:

Begin the lesson by distributing paper and pens to each student. Ask them to draw faces showing people with different feelings. They may draw people who are excited, proud, happy, joyful, relieved, and celebrating. Say, "Have you ever had any of these feelings? How do you think the Israelites felt when David defeated Goliath? Let's find out!"

3. Review key vocabulary:

- **SWORD:** A long, sharp weapon used in battles, with a handle and a blade
- **GATH:** A city where Goliath, the giant that David fought, was from
- **JONATHAN:** The son of King Saul and David's best friend
- **TAMBOURINE:** A musical instrument that you shake or hit, made of a frame with small metal discs that jingle
- **JESSE:** David's father

4. Bible memory verse to help children remember God's Word:

"David went out and was successful wherever Saul sent him, so that Saul set him over the men of war." (1 Samuel 18:5)

5. Read 1 Samuel 17:50-18:7 or read the Bible story below:

With just a sling and a stone, David struck Goliath on the forehead, and the giant fell. David had no sword, so he ran to Goliath, took the giant's sword, and used it to finish him. When the Philistines saw their champion was dead, they fled in fear. The men of Israel and Judah cheered and chased the Philistines all the way to their cities, wounding many along the way. Afterward, the Israelites returned and collected valuables from the Philistine camp. David took Goliath's head to Jerusalem and kept the giant's armor in his tent. King Saul watched the battle. He asked his commander, Abner, "Who is this young man's father?" Abner didn't know, so Saul asked to meet David. When David came before the king, holding Goliath's head, Saul asked, "Whose son are you?" David replied, "I am the son of Jesse, from Bethlehem." Jonathan, Saul's son, met David and they became best friends. Jonathan gave David his robe, armor, sword, bow, and belt. King Saul made David a leader in his army. Everyone was pleased with David. When David and Saul returned from battle, women from Israel sang, "Saul has killed his thousands, but David his tens of thousands."

6. Let's review:

1. Let's review:
2. What was today's story about?
3. How did David defeat Goliath?
4. What did David do after he killed Goliath?
5. How did King Saul react to David's victory over Goliath?
6. Who became best friends with David after his victory?
7. What special gift did Jonathan give to David?
8. How did the people of Israel react to David's success in battle?
9. What song did the women sing to celebrate David's victory?

7. Activites:

* Coloring page: Israel celebrates
* Bible quiz: Israel celebrates
* Newspaper worksheet: Shepherd defeats giant!
* Worksheet: Heroes and villains
* Fill in the Blanks: Run away!
* Worksheet: David and Jonathan
* Worksheets: King of the Israelites
* Worksheet: Who was David?
* Creative writing: The day I defeated Goliath
* Craft activity: Celebrate David's victory over Goliath
* Let's learn Hebrew: Tribe of Judah
* Bible story activity: Write your own story of David & Goliath

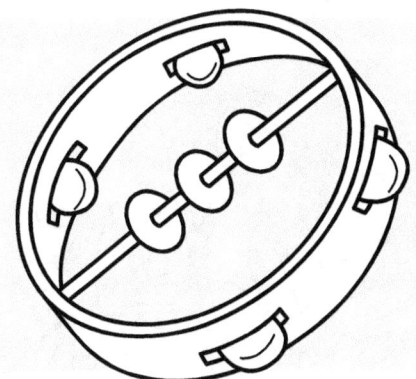

"Saul has struck down his thousands, and David his ten thousands."

(1 Samuel 18:7)

Israel CELEBRATES

Read 1 Samuel 17:50-18:7. Answer the questions below.

1. What did David use to defeat Goliath?
2. What did David do after Goliath fell to the ground?
3. What happened to the Philistines when they saw that Goliath was dead?
4. Who chased the Philistines after Goliath was defeated?
5. What did the Israelites do after returning from chasing the Philistines?
6. Where did David take Goliath's head?
7. Who asked about David's family after he defeated Goliath?
8. What did King Saul ask David when he met him?
9. Who became best friends with David after he defeated Goliath?
10. What special items did Jonathan give to David?

City of Jerusalem

The Jerusalem Times

1 SAMUEL 18   LAND OF ISRAEL   A BIBLE HISTORY PUBLICATION

Israel celebrates

Shepherd defeats giant!

Slings for sale

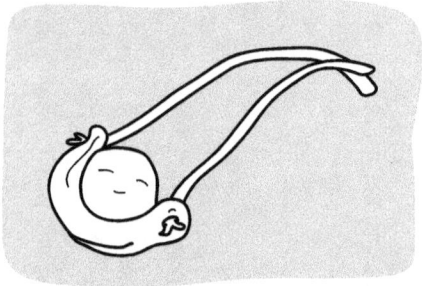

Heroes and villains

Read 1 Samuel 15:1-18:7. The story of David and Goliath features four important Bible characters: David, Goliath, King Saul, and the prophet Samuel. For each character, fill in information about their role in the story.

Role: ....
....
....

DAVID

Role: ....
....
....

GOLIATH

Role: ....
....
....

KING SAUL

Role: ....
....
....

SAMUEL

Run away!

Read 1 Samuel 17:51-53 (ESV). Fill in the blanks. Color the fleeing Philistine.

" David ran and stood over the .... and took his sword and drew it out of its .... and killed him and cut off his head with it. When the Philistines saw that their champion was dead, they fled. The men of .... and .... rose with a .... and pursued the Philistines as far as Gath and the gates of Ekron, so that the wounded Philistines fell on the way from .... as far as Gath and .... And the people of Israel came back from chasing the Philistines, and they plundered their camp. "

Read 1 Samuel 17:55-18:5. Imagine yourself as Jonathan.

Write a short paragraph describing why you made a covenant with David, and why you gave him your sword and clothing.

....

....

....

....

....

....

....

King of the Israelites

This article explains how King Saul was appointed king and how he ruled Israel. Read the text and answer the questions on the next page.

For centuries, the people of Israel were governed by local leaders known as "judges." Because some judges became dishonest, the Israelites asked the prophet Samuel to choose a king to lead them. Despite God's warning about the dangers of having a king, Saul was chosen to lead Israel. He created a base in the town of Gibeah (the main town of the tribe of Benjamin), a royal administration, and an army to fight their enemies.

Saul's reign began well. He was a strong warrior whose army defeated the Ammonites, Moabites, Edomites, and Amalekites. However, it was not long before King Saul began to disobey God. For example, rather than trust God for victory against the Philistines, he made a sacrifice to God instead of waiting for Samuel to do it. He disobeyed God again by holding the king of the Amalekites prisoner and keeping much of their livestock. Later, Saul became jealous of David and tried to kill him many times. To make things worse, he murdered the High Priest. No wonder God stopped talking to Saul!

Archaeologists have identified Saul's hometown of Gibeah with the ancient ruins on a hill known today as Tel el-Ful, three miles north of Jerusalem. Excavations from 1922 to 1923 show that the site of Gibeah was inhabited around 1100 BC, during the time of King Saul. Saul's simple rustic fortress was found here. Archaeologists discovered the main building was built more like a dungeon than a royal palace, with massive stone construction and deep walls.

King of the Israelites

Why did the Israelites ask the prophet Samuel to choose a king?
....
....
....
....
....

Where did King Saul create his base and royal administration?
....
....
....

Why did God stop talking to Saul?
....
....
....
....

What were some of King Saul's early successes as a warrior?
....
....
....
....
....
....

Draw King Saul.

Who was David?

Read 1 Samuel 16:1-18:16. Complete the worksheet below.

Hometown:

....

David is most famous for:

....

David was of the tribe of:

....

Write three character traits that describe David. Give an example from the Bible for each trait:

1. ....

2. ....

3. ....

Draw a picture of David the soldier:

JUDAH

Celebrate David's victory

Imagine you are an Israelite in ancient Israel. Use this worksheet to create a party invitation to celebrate David's victory over Goliath. Research life in ancient Israel, and then fill in the details below. Add them to your invitation on the next page. Color your invitation.

Information to add to the invitation:

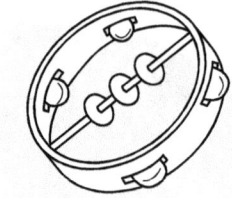

1. Date and Time:

   When: ....

2. Location:

   Where: ....

3. Host:

   Hosted by: ....

4. Special Guests:

   Special Guests: ....

5. Message:

   ....

   ....

   ....

Yehudah

The Hebrew name for Judah is Yehudah. Judah was the fourth son of Jacob (Israel). Jacob blessed Judah, saying, "Your brothers shall praise you; your hand shall be on the neck of your enemies; your father's sons shall bow down before you. Judah is a lion's cub; from the prey, my son, you have gone up... The scepter shall not depart from Judah, nor the ruler's staff from between his feet..." (Genesis 49:8-10). David, one of the most famous members of the tribe of Judah, became the second king of Israel. He was chosen by God and anointed by the prophet Samuel. David's lineage is significant because it was prophesied that the Messiah would come from his bloodline. This prophecy was fulfilled in Yeshua, who is a descendant of David. Other famous people from the tribe of Judah include Caleb and King Solomon, David's son, who built the first Temple in Jerusalem.

www.biblepathwayadventures.com
The story of David & Goliath Activity Book
© BPA Publishing Ltd 2024

Let's write!

Practice writing Judah's Hebrew name on the lines below.

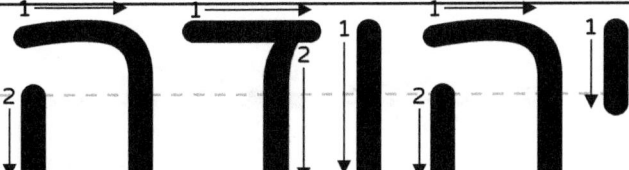

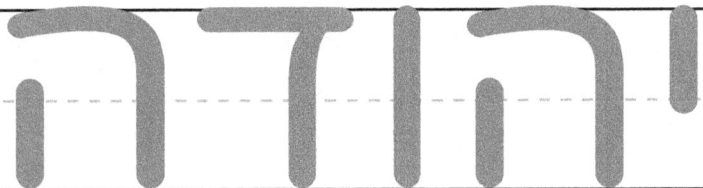

Try this on your own.
Remember that Hebrew is read from RIGHT to LEFT.

Write your own story of David & Goliath

Read 1 Samuel 16:1-18:7. Beside each picture, write the story of David and Goliath in your own words. Then, color the pictures.

....

....

....

....

....

....

....

....

....

....

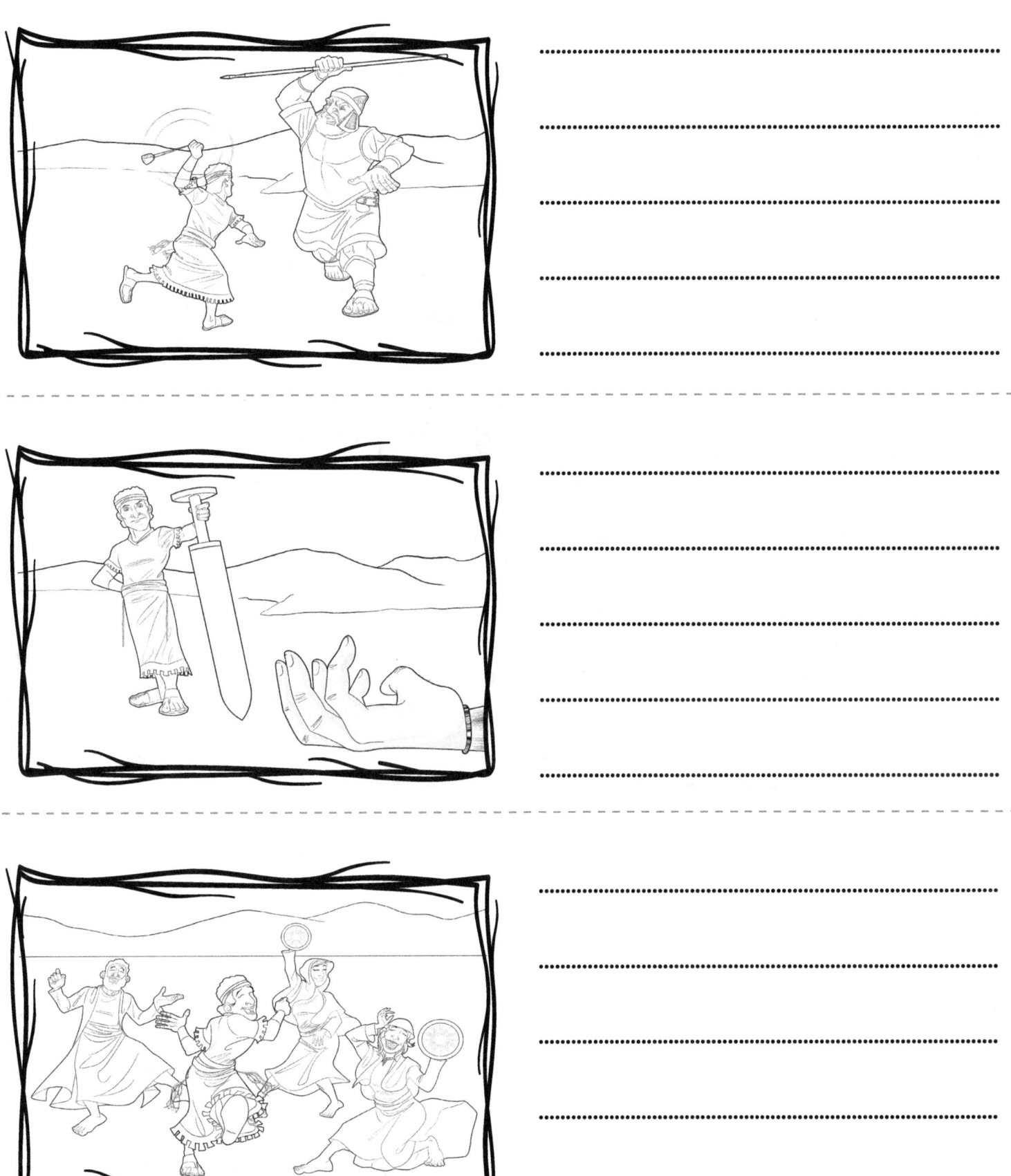

Bible story cards

The story of David & Goliath

Samuel Anoints David

Samuel took the horn of oil and anointed him in the midst of his brothers. And the Spirit of God rushed upon David from that day forward.

1 Samuel 16:13

 1 Samuel 16:1-13

David in Saul's Service

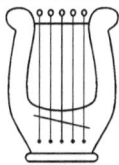

Whenever the harmful spirit from God was upon Saul, David took the lyre and played it with his hand. So, Saul was refreshed and was well, and the harmful spirit departed from him.

1 Samuel 16:23

 1 Samuel 16:14-23

Goliath's Challenge

And there came out from the camp of the Philistines a champion named Goliath of Gath, whose height was six cubits and a span. He had a helmet of bronze on his head, and he was armed with a coat of mail, and the weight of the coat was five thousand shekels of bronze. And he had bronze armor on his legs, and a javelin of bronze slung between his shoulders. The shaft of his spear was like a weaver's beam, and his spear's head weighed six hundred shekels of iron.

1 Samuel 17:4-7

 1 Samuel 17:1-11

Jesse's Instructions

Jesse said to David, "Take for your brothers an ephah of this parched grain, and these ten loaves, and carry them quickly to the camp to your brothers. Also take these ten cheeses to the commander of their thousand. See if your brothers are well, and bring some token from them."

1 Samuel 17:17-18

 1 Samuel 17:12-19

David at the Battlefield

David rose early in the morning and left the sheep with a keeper and took the provisions and went, as Jesse had commanded him. And he came to the encampment as the host was going out to the battle line, shouting the war cry.

1 Samuel 17:20

📖 1 Samuel 17:20-30

David Volunteers to Fight

David said, "Yahweh who delivered me from the paw of the lion and from the paw of the bear will deliver me from the hand of this Philistine." Saul said to David, "Go, and God be with you!"

1 Samuel 17:37

📖 1 Samuel 17:31-37

David Prepares for Battle

David said to Saul, "I cannot go with these, for I have not tested them." He put them off. Then he took his staff in his hand and chose five smooth stones from the brook and put them in his shepherd's pouch. His sling was in his hand, and he approached the Philistine.

1 Samuel 17:39-40

📖 1 Samuel 17:38-40

David Faces Goliath

Goliath moved forward and came near to David, with his shield-bearer in front of him. And when the Philistine looked and saw David, he disdained him, for he was but a youth, ruddy and handsome in appearance.

1 Samuel 17:41-42

📖 1 Samuel 17:41-47

Bible Pathway Adventures

David Slays Goliath

David put his hand in his bag and took out a stone and slung it and struck the Philistine on his forehead. The stone sank into his forehead, and he fell on his face to the ground. So, David prevailed over the Philistine with a sling and with a stone, and struck the Philistine and killed him.

1 Samuel 17:49-50

 1 Samuel 17:48-54

Saul Questions David

Saul said to him, "Whose son are you, young man?" And David answered, "I am the son of your servant Jesse the Bethlehemite."

1 Samuel 17:58

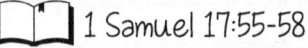 1 Samuel 17:55-58

David and Jonathan

Jonathan made a covenant with David, because he loved him as his own soul. He stripped himself of the robe that was on him and gave it to David, and his armor, and even his sword and his bow and his belt.

1 Samuel 18:3-4

 1 Samuel 18:1-4

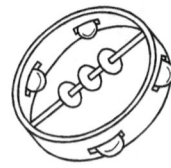

Israel Celebrates!

As they were coming home, when David returned from striking down the Philistine, the women came out of all the cities of Israel, singing and dancing, to meet King Saul, with tambourines, with songs of joy, and with musical instruments.

1 Samuel 18:6

 1 Samuel 18:5-9

Crafts & Projects

Samuel meets David

Read 1 Samuel 16:1-13. Color and cut out the people.
Paste them inside the house.

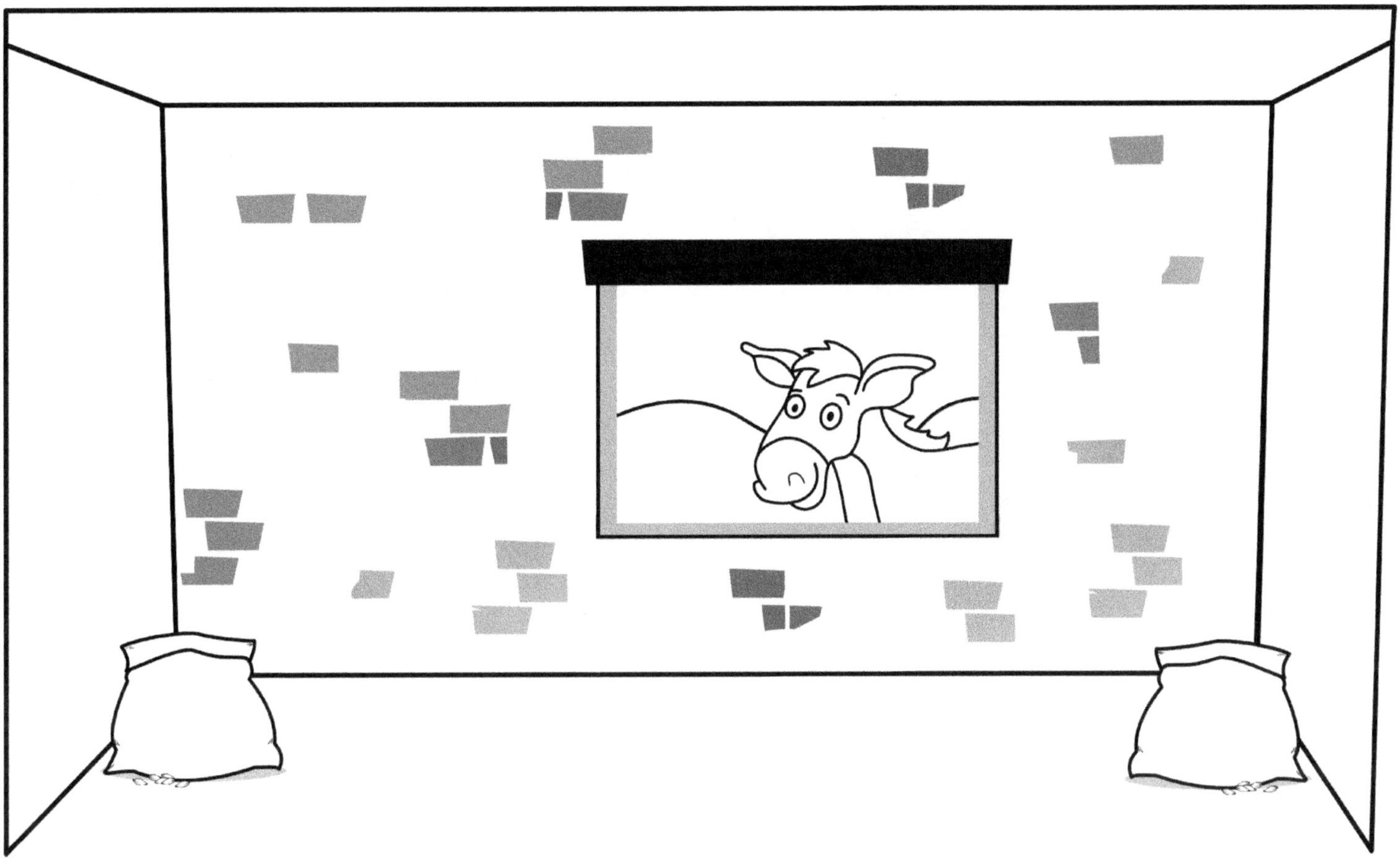

Brother David Samuel Jesse

Make your own lyre

You will need:

1. Heavy cardstock
2. School glue
3. Tape
4. Black string or yarn
5. Felt pens, crayons, tissue paper, glitter, or colored pencils

Instructions:

1. Print or copy the lyre template onto heavy cardstock. Cut out the template and decorate the lyre.
2. Tape five pieces of string or yarn onto the lyre template.
3. Glue both sides of the template together to create a lyre.

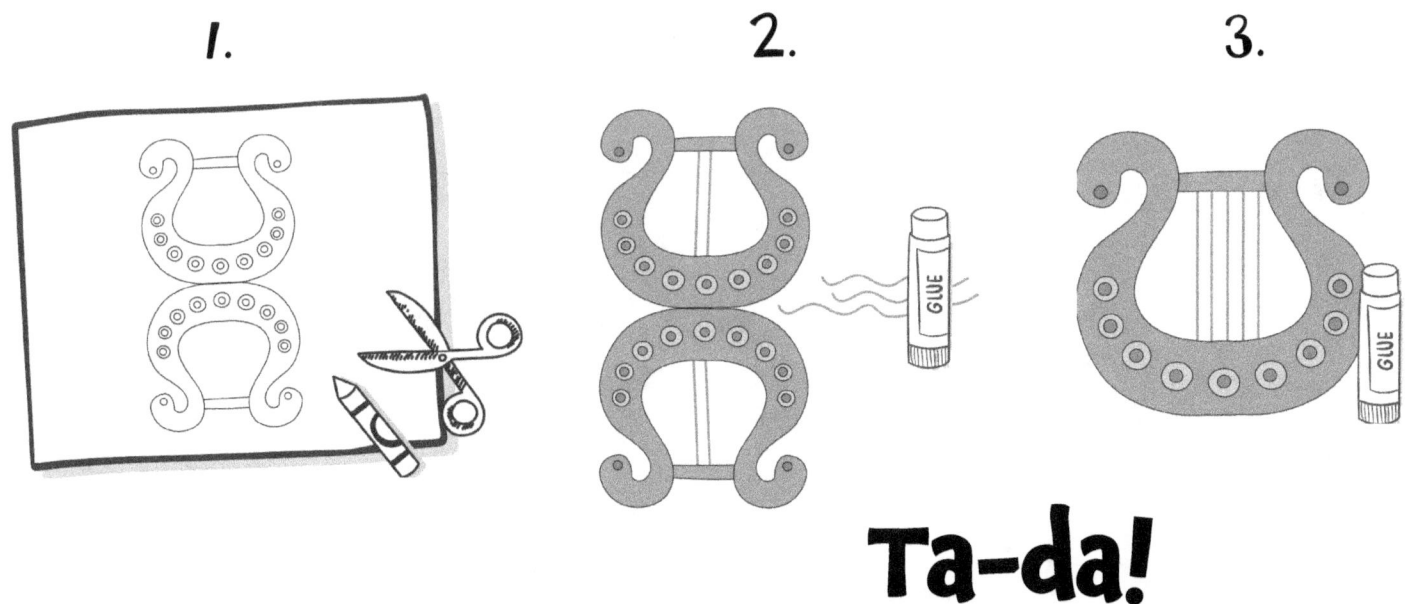

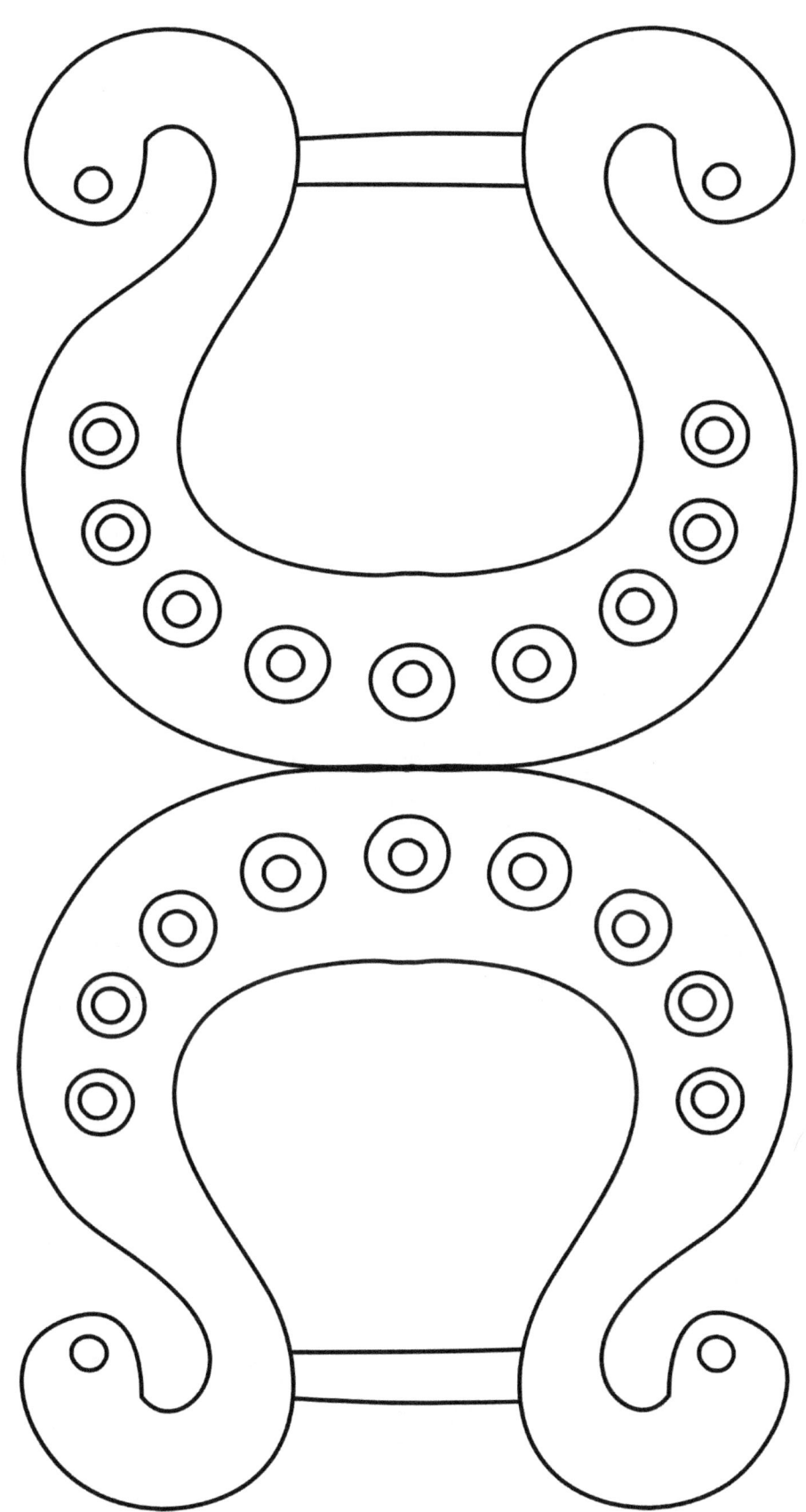

Who said it?

Read 1 Samuel 15-16.
Color and cut out each Bible character.
Match the quote with the person who said it.

1. "I defy the armies of Israel. Give me a man so we may fight together."
 - 1 Samuel 17:10

2. "For who is this uncircumcised Philistine, that he should defy the armies of the living God?"
 - 1 Samuel 17:26

3. "Please let David stand before me, for he has found favor in my sight."
 - 1 Samuel 16:22

4. "…you have rejected the word of God and He has rejected you from being king over Israel."
 - 1 Samuel 15:26

David   Goliath   King Saul   Samuel

Make a slingshot!

You will need:
1. Colored card stock
2. Paint, felt pens, or crayons
3. Pipe cleaners
4. School glue and glue sticks
5. Wooden craft sticks

Preparation: Cut out five 'stones' from the template on the next page.

Instructions:

1. Ask children to color the paper 'stones' gray or brown.
2. Give children a piece of colored cardstock. Take three wooden craft sticks and glue one craft stick to the bottom center of the cardstock.
3. Wrap a brown pipe cleaner around two wooden craft sticks.
4. Place school glue onto the back of the two craft sticks and glue them in a Y shape at the top of the third craft stick.
5. Glue the five stones on the cardstock around the slingshot.

1.

2.
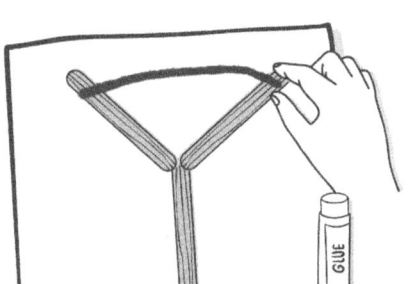

3.

Ta-da!

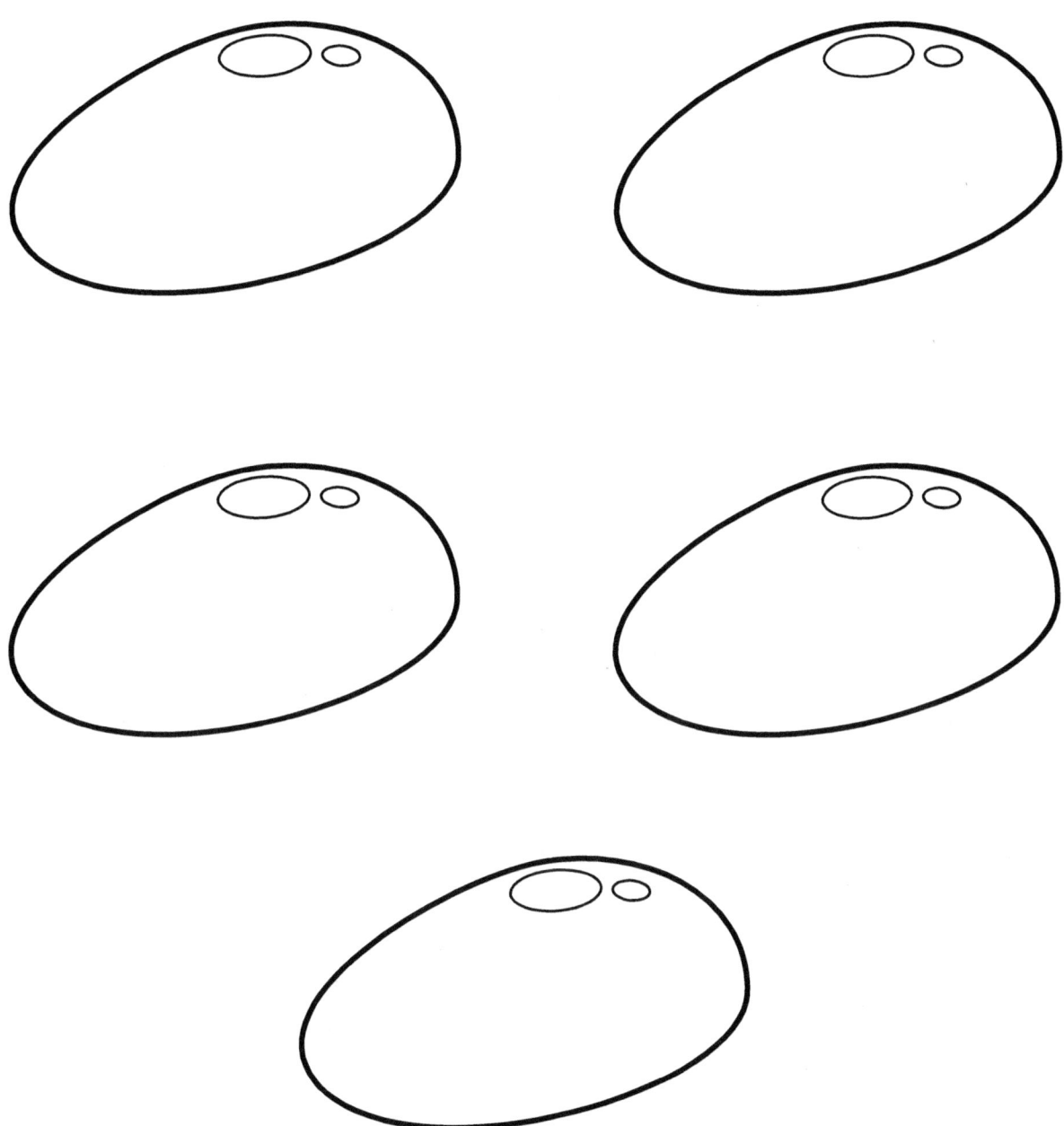

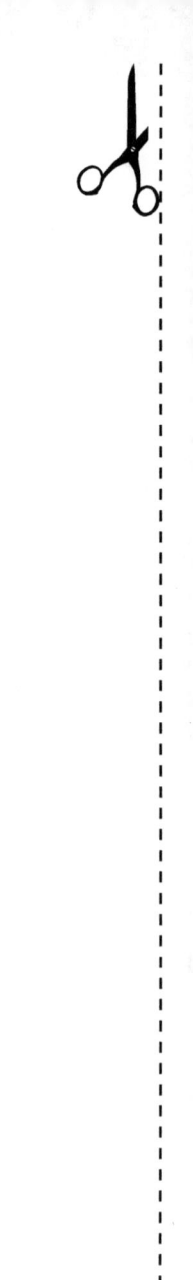

Answer Key

Lesson One: David is anointed king
Let's Review:
1. The story was about King Saul disobeying God's command and God choosing David as the next king
2. God commanded King Saul to destroy everything in the Amalekite city
3. No, King Saul did not fully obey God's command. He kept the best animals and spared the Amalekite king
4. Samuel was very upset when he learned that Saul did not fully obey God
5. Because Saul disobeyed Him, God decided to choose a new king
6. God sent Samuel to the house of Jesse in Bethlehem to find the next king of Israel
7. God chose David because He looks at the heart, not the appearance
8. After Samuel anointed David as the next king of Israel, the Spirit of God was with David

Worksheet: Who were the Amalekites?
1. The Amalekites lived in tents made of wool and goat's hair, traveled on camels, and moved around a lot
2. King Saul did not fully obey God's instructions; he kept some of the best animals and took the Amalekite king as a prisoner

Worksheet: Saul spares King Agag
1. God told Saul to strike the Amalekites and devote to destruction all that they have, sparing no one and nothing, including men, women, children, infants, and animals (oxen, sheep, camels, and donkeys)
2. Saul disobeyed God by sparing Agag, the king of the Amalekites, and the best of the sheep, oxen, fattened calves, lambs, and all that was good, instead of utterly destroying everything as he was instructed
3. Saul told the Kenites to leave the Amalekites before the attack because the Kenites had shown kindness to the people of Israel when they came up out of Egypt, and Saul did not want to destroy them along with the Amalekites

Bible quiz: The prophet Samuel
1. Samuel thought it was Eli calling him
2. Samuel's mother brought him a new robe each year
3. Samuel never cut his hair because he was dedicated to God as a Nazarite
4. The Israelites demanded a king from Samuel

5. Samuel warned the Israelites that a king would take their sons and daughters, their best fields, vineyards, and olive groves, and a tenth of their grain and flocks
6. Samuel anointed Saul as the first king of the Israelites
7. Samuel lived in the land of Ephraim, but his family belonged to the tribe of Levi
8. The names of Samuel's two sons were Joel and Abijah
9. Samuel's jobs were being a prophet, judge, priest, and army commander
10. When Samuel rose from the grave, he told Saul that the Lord had departed from him and that Saul and his sons would die in battle the next day

Worksheet: David the shepherd
1. David's hometown was Bethlehem
2. Ask children to answer this question. Answers may vary
3. The names of David's brothers were Eliab, Abinadab, Shammah (also called Shimea or Shimeah in some translations), Nethanel, Raddai, and Ozem
4. Ask children to answer this question. Answers may vary

Worksheet: David is chosen king
God said to Samuel, "Do not look at his appearance or at his physical stature, because I have refused him. For God does not see as man sees. Man looks at the outward appearance but I look at the heart." So, Jesse called Abinadab and made him pass before Samuel. And he said, "Neither has Yahweh chosen this one." Then Jesse made Shammah pass by. And he said, "Neither has God chosen this one." Jesse made seven of his sons pass before Samuel. And Samuel said to Jesse, "God has not chosen these." And Samuel said to Jesse, "Are all the young men here?" Then he said, "There is still the youngest, and he is keeping the sheep." Samuel said to Jesse, "Bring him here. For we will not sit down till he comes here." So, he sent and brought David in. Now he was ruddy, with bright eyes and good-looking. And God said, "Arise, anoint him; for this is the one!" Then Samuel took the horn of oil and anointed David in the midst of his brothers. And the Spirit of God came upon David from that day forward.

Worksheet: Discovering Bethlehem
1. Jacob buried Rachel near Bethlehem (Genesis 48:7)
2. Naomi and Ruth returned to Bethlehem (Ruth 1:19)
3. Samuel found David in Bethlehem (1 Samuel 16:12-13)
4. King Herod ordered male babies in Bethlehem under two years old to be killed (Matthew 2:16)

Worksheet: Jesse's family
1. Sons: Eliab, Abinadab, Shimea, Nethanel, Raddai, Ozem, and David. The Bible does not tell us the name of Jesse's eighth son
2. Daughters: Zeruiah and Abigail

Lesson Two: David works for King Saul
Let's Review:
1. The story was about how David helped King Saul by playing the lyre to make him feel better
2. When the Spirit of God left him, King Saul was troubled by a harmful spirit
3. Saul's servants suggested finding someone who could play the lyre well to help him feel better
4. One of the young men suggested David, the son of Jesse from Bethlehem, to play the lyre for Saul
5. Jesse sent a donkey loaded with bread, a skin of wine, and a young goat with David to King Saul
6. When David arrived at Saul's palace, he took on the role of Saul's armor-bearer
7. Saul loved David greatly and was pleased with him
8. Whenever David played the lyre, Saul felt refreshed and well, and the harmful spirit left him

Bible word search puzzle: David works for King Saul

Worksheet: Who was King Saul?
1. David helped calm King Saul by playing the lyre (a small harp). The soothing music made Saul feel better and drove away the harmful spirit that troubled him
2. King Saul became jealous of David because David gained fame and admiration after defeating the giant Goliath and was successful in many battles. The people praised David more than Saul, which made Saul envious. Because of his jealousy, Saul tried to kill David several times, but David always managed to escape

Map activity: Tribe of Benjamin
1. The tribe of Benjamin had several advantages because of their location in Israel. Their land had access to the Jordan River and the Dead Sea, which allowed for lots of trade. The eastern part of their land was good for farming, providing them with agricultural resources. Additionally, the mountains in the middle of their territory offered protection from enemies, making it a secure area
2. Despite its small size, the territory of the tribe of Benjamin was important due to its strategic location. It was situated between two key areas: Ephraim to the north and Judah to the south. This central position allowed them to interact and trade with neighboring tribes effectively. The combination of trade access, fertile land, and natural protection made the territory of Benjamin a valuable and significant area within Israel

Worksheet: David plays the lyre
1. The servants believed that music would help Saul feel better when the evil spirit from God tormented him (1 Samuel 16:16)
2. The servant recommended David, the son of Jesse from Bethlehem, because he knew how to play the lyre, was brave, a warrior, spoke well, and was a fine-looking man who had God with him (1 Samuel 16:18)
3. When David played the lyre, relief would come to Saul; he would feel better, and the evil spirit would leave him (1 Samuel 16:23)

Lesson Three: Facing Goliath
Let's Review:
1. The story was about the Philistines and Israelites preparing for battle and the challenge from the giant Goliath
2. They gathered at Socoh, which belongs to Judah, and camped in the Valley of Elah
3. The giant warrior was Goliath from Gath
4. Goliath had a bronze helmet, a coat of mail, bronze armor on his legs, a bronze javelin, and a large spear with an iron spearhead
5. Goliath challenged the Israelites to send out a man to fight him, saying the winner's people would serve the other
6. King Saul and the Israelites were dismayed and greatly afraid
7. Goliath came out and challenged the Israelites for forty days
8. David was the youngest son of Jesse from Bethlehem, and he was tending his father's sheep during this time

Bible quiz: Facing Goliath
1. Goliath lived in the Philistine town of Gath
2. Goliath challenged the Israelites to a fight for forty days
3. The Israelite army feared Goliath because of his enormous size, strength, and intimidating appearance

4. Goliath's armor was made from bronze
5. Goliath was about 9.5 feet tall
6. David, a young shepherd boy, challenged Goliath to a fight
7. Goliath's armor plate weighed five thousand shekels of bronze, which is approximately 125 pounds
8. David killed Goliath with a sling and a stone, hitting him in the forehead and causing him to fall to the ground. He then chopped off his head with a sword
9. The Philistine and Israelite soldiers faced each other in the Valley of Elah
10. We read about Goliath in the Bible in 1 Samuel 17

Worksheet: The Nephilim
1. The Nephilim were a race of giants and superheroes known for doing acts of great evil, produced by the union of fallen angels and human women (Genesis 6:1-4)
2. Some of the Nephilim were up to 20 feet tall, with skeletons found that measured seventeen feet, twelve feet, and fourteen to sixteen feet tall
3. Some Nephilim had unusual physical characteristics such as double rows of teeth and six fingers or toes on each hand or foot (2 Samuel 21:20)
4. The most famous Nephilim was Goliath of Gath, who was faced by the Israelite soldiers

Worksheet: Match the scriptures
"There came out from the camp of the Philistines a champion named Goliath of Gath, whose height was six cubits and a span." (1 Samuel 17:4)
"Why have you come out to draw up for battle? Am I not a Philistine, and are you not servants of Saul? Choose a man for yourselves, and let him come down to me." (1 Samuel 17:8)
"When Saul and all Israel heard these words of the Philistine, they were dismayed and greatly afraid." (1 Samuel 17:11)
"For forty days the Philistine came forward and took his stand, morning and evening." (1 Samuel 17:16)

Worksheet: Valley of Elah
1. The Philistine army positioned themselves on the western slopes near Azekah, while King Saul and his army camped in the high country on the eastern side of the valley closer to Socoh
2. "Representational combat" was a system where two heroes fought on behalf of their respective armies, and the winner claimed victory for their tribe or nation. This system helped avoid many deaths on both sides
3. Ask children to answer this question. Answers may vary

Worksheet: Who said it?
1 = Goliath, 2 = David, 3 = King Saul 4 = Samuel

Bible verse puzzle: How big was Goliath?
There came out from the camp of the Philistines a champion named Goliath of Gath whose height was six cubits and a span

Worksheet: Who was Goliath?
1. Goliath was from Gath
2. Goliath was about 9.5 feet tall
3. Goliath wore bronze armor, including a helmet, a coat of mail, bronze armor on his legs, and carried a large spear
4. Goliath is more famous for challenging the Israelite army and being defeated by David with a sling and a stone

Lesson Four: David fights Goliath
Let's Review:
1. The story was about David fighting Goliath
2. The two main characters were David and Goliath
3. Goliath was about 9 feet tall
4. David chose five small stones and a slingshot
5. The Israelites were filled with fear when they saw Goliath
6. Goliath taunted David, saying he was just a boy coming at him with sticks
7. David responded by saying he came in the name of Yahweh, and that God would deliver Goliath into his hands
8. David used his slingshot to hit Goliath in the forehead, causing him to fall, and then David defeated him

Bible word search puzzle: Defeating the giant

Worksheet: Who were the Philistines?
1. The Philistines originally came from the Aegean region, possibly from the island of Crete, and they inhabited five main cities: Gaza, Ashkelon, Ashdod, Gath, and Ekron
2. The Israelites went to the Philistines to get their weapons sharpened because there were no blacksmiths in Israel, as the Philistines did not allow the Hebrews to make swords or spears (1 Samuel 13:19-20)

Bible word scramble: How did David defeat Goliath?
David prevailed over the Philistine with a sling and with a stone.

Worksheet: Facing the giant
David said to Goliath, "You come to me with a sword and with a spear and with a javelin, but I come to you in the name of Yahweh, the God of the armies of Israel, whom you have defied. This day God will deliver you into my hand, and I will strike you down and cut off your head. I will give the dead bodies of the host of the Philistines this day to the birds of the air and to the wild beasts of the earth, that all the earth may know that there is a God in Israel, and that all this assembly may know that God saves not with sword and spear. For the battle is God's, and He will give you into our hand." When Goliath arose and drew near to meet David, David ran quickly toward the battle line to meet him. He put his hand in his bag and took out a stone and slung it and struck the Philistine on his forehead. The stone sank into his forehead, and he fell on his face to the ground. David prevailed over Goliath with a sling and with a stone, and struck the Philistine and killed him.

Bible crossword: David fights the Philistine

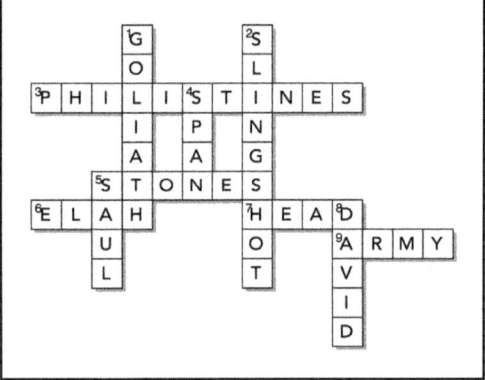

Worksheet: David and Goliath
1. Goliath was over nine feet tall
2. David wore his regular clothes; he did not wear armor
3. David killed Goliath with a slingshot and a stone

Lesson Five: Israel celebrates!
Let's Review:
1. The story was about David defeating Goliath and how the people of Israel celebrated
2. David defeated Goliath with a sling and a stone, hitting him in the forehead
3. After he killed Goliath, David took Goliath's sword and cut off his head
4. King Saul was curious about David's family background
5. Jonathan, King Saul's son, became best friends with David
6. Jonathan gave David his robe, armor, sword, bow, and belt as a sign of their friendship
7. The people of Israel celebrated David's success with great joy
8. The women sang, "Saul has slain his thousands, and David his tens of thousands."

Bible quiz: Israel celebrates
1. David used a slingshot and a stone to defeat Goliath
2. After Goliath fell to the ground, David took Goliath's sword and killed him
3. When the Philistines saw that Goliath was dead, they fled in fear
4. The men of Israel and Judah chased the Philistines after Goliath was defeated
5. After returning from chasing the Philistines, the Israelites collected valuables from the Philistine camp
6. David took Goliath's head to Jerusalem
7. King Saul asked about David's family after he defeated Goliath
8. When King Saul met David, he asked, "Whose son are you?"
9. Jonathan, King Saul's son, became best friends with David after he defeated Goliath
10. Jonathan gave David his robe, armor, sword, bow, and belt as a sign of their friendship

Worksheet: Heroes and villains
1. David
   David is a young shepherd boy who bravely volunteers to fight the giant Goliath. Even though he is young and has no experience in battle, David trusts God to help him. He uses a slingshot and a stone to defeat Goliath with a single shot

2. Goliath
   Goliath is a giant warrior from the Philistines who is very strong and scary. He challenges the Israelites to send someone to fight him, and he makes them very afraid. Goliath keeps taunting the Israelites until David steps up to face him. David defeats Goliath with a slingshot and a stone, which causes the Philistines to run away in fear

3. King Saul
   King Saul is the first king of Israel. He leads his people in battles, but he often disobeys God's commands. In this story, Saul is afraid of Goliath and doesn't know what to do. When David defeats Goliath, Saul becomes jealous and afraid of David because everyone starts to like David more

4. Samuel
   Samuel is a prophet who speaks for God and helps guide the people of Israel. He tells Saul when he has done wrong and helps the people understand God's plans. Samuel also anoints David to be the next king after Saul

Fill in the Blanks: Run away!
David ran and stood over the Philistine and took his sword and drew it out of its sheath and killed him and cut off his head with it. When the Philistines saw that their champion was dead, they fled. The men of Israel and Judah rose with a shout and pursued the Philistines as far as Gath and the gates of Ekron, so that the wounded Philistines fell on the way from Shaaraim as far as Gath and Ekron. And the people of Israel came back from chasing the Philistines, and they plundered their camp.

Worksheet: King of the Israelites
1. The Israelites asked the prophet Samuel to choose a king because some judges had become dishonest
2. King Saul created his base and royal administration in the town of Gibeah
3. King Saul's early successes as a warrior included defeating the Ammonites, Moabites, Edomites, and Amalekites
4. God stopped talking to Saul because he disobeyed God multiple times, including making a sacrifice without waiting for Samuel, keeping the Amalekite king and livestock, becoming jealous of David and trying to kill him, and murdering the High Priest

Worksheet: Who was David?
1. David's hometown was Bethlehem
2. David is most famous for defeating Goliath
3. David was of the tribe of Judah, one of the 12 tribes of Israel
4. Example character traits:
   a. Brave: David showed bravery by facing and defeating Goliath with only a slingshot and a stone (1 Samuel 17:45-49)
   b. Faithful: David demonstrated his faithfulness to God by trusting Him completely during his battle with Goliath and throughout his life (1 Samuel 17:37)
   c. Loyal: David exhibited loyalty to King Saul, even when Saul sought to kill him, by sparing Saul's life when he had the chance to take it (1 Samuel 24:10)

◊ Discover more Activity Books! ◊

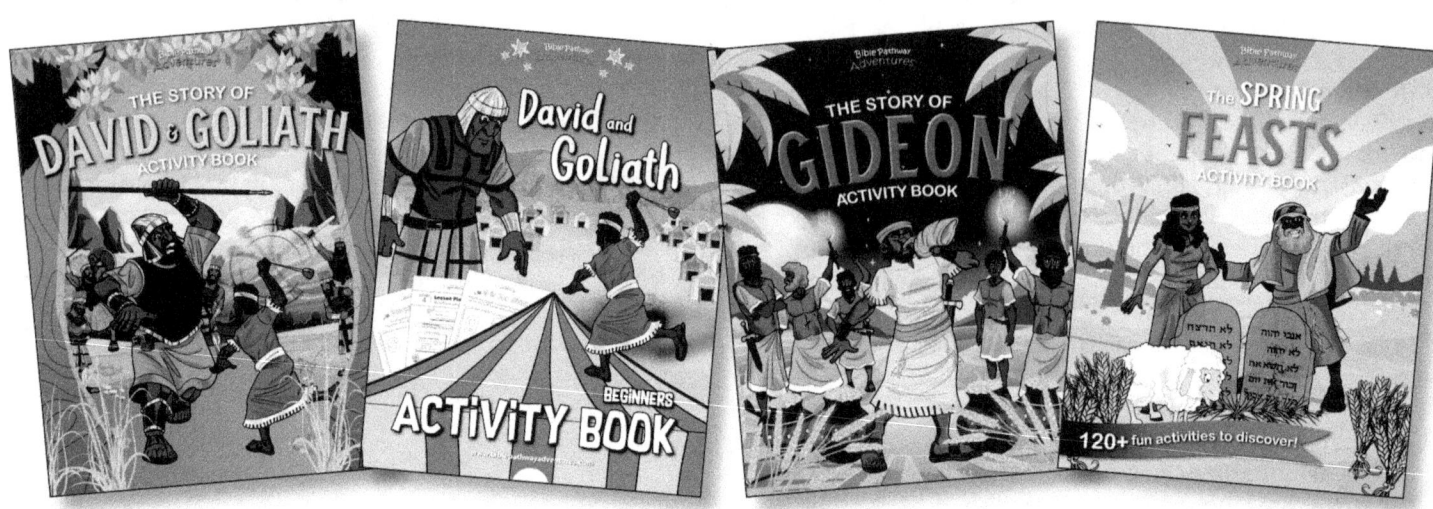

Available for purchase at www.biblepathwayadventures.com

INSTANT DOWNLOAD!

David and Goliath
David and Goliath (Beginners)
The Story of Gideon
The Spring Feasts

Favorite Bible Stories
The Passover & Unleavened Bread
Moses and the Ten Plagues
The Faith of Abraham

www.ingramcontent.com/pod-product-compliance
Lightning Source LLC
LaVergne TN
LVHW081530060526
838200LV00049B/2267